365 Yummy Cold Beverage Recipes

(365 Yummy Cold Beverage Recipes - Volume 1)

Tracy Yost

Copyright: Published in the United States by Tracy Yost/ © TRACY YOST

Published on December, 02 2020

All rights reserved. No part of this publication may be reproduced, stored in retrieval system, copied in any form or by any means, electronic, mechanical, photocopying, recording or otherwise transmitted without written permission from the publisher. Please do not participate in or encourage piracy of this material in any way. You must not circulate this book in any format. TRACY YOST does not control or direct users' actions and is not responsible for the information or content shared, harm and/or actions of the book readers.

In accordance with the U.S. Copyright Act of 1976, the scanning, uploading and electronic sharing of any part of this book without the permission of the publisher constitute unlawful piracy and theft of the author's intellectual property. If you would like to use material from the book (other than just simply for reviewing the book), prior permission must be obtained by contacting the author at publishing@crumblerecipes.com

Thank you for your support of the author's rights.

Content

365 AWESOME COLD BEVERAGE RECIPES 8

1. Almond Lemonade Tea 8
2. American Beauty 8
3. Apple Brandy 8
4. Apple Cider Sipper 9
5. Apple Grape Drink 9
6. Apple Martini 9
7. Apple Pie In A Glass 10
8. Apricot Brandy Slush 10
9. Apricot Peach Smoothies 11
10. Baby Shower Punch 11
11. Banana Breakfast Smoothies 11
12. Banana Cocoa Smoothies 12
13. Banana Coffee Smoothie 12
14. Banana Milk Drink 12
15. Banana Mixed Berry Smoothie 13
16. Banana Nog 13
17. Banana Pineapple Slush 14
18. Banana Split Smoothies 14
19. Banana Strawberry Smoothies 15
20. Banana And Chocolate Smoothie 15
21. Banana Almond Milk Shakes 15
22. Basil Citrus Cocktail 16
23. Basil Tomato Juice 16
24. Beer Margaritas 17
25. Bella Basil Raspberry Tea 17
26. Berry Banana Smoothies 17
27. Berry Breakfast Smoothies 18
28. Berry Delicious Smoothies 18
29. Berry Fruity Punch 18
30. Berry Nutritious Smoothies 19
31. Berry Slush 19
32. Berry Smoothie 20
33. Berry Smoothies 20
34. Berry Splash Smoothies 20
35. Berry Yogurt Shakes 21
36. Black Eyed Susan 21
37. Blackberry Banana Smoothies 22
38. Blackberry Brandy Slush 22
39. Blackberry Lemonade 22
40. Blended Fruit Chiller 23
41. Blueberry Banana Smoothies 23
42. Blueberry Fruit Smoothie 23
43. Blueberry Mango Smoothies 24
44. Blueberry Milk Shake 24
45. Blueberry Orange Blast 25
46. Blueberry Orange Smoothies 25
47. Blueberry Oat Smoothies 25
48. Bourbon Slush 26
49. Brandy Slush 26
50. Breakfast Wassail 26
51. Buttermilk Boost 27
52. Buttermilk Ice Cream Shake 27
53. Buttermilk Shake 28
54. Candy Apple Martini 28
55. Cantaloupe Banana Smoothies 28
56. Cantaloupe Orange Milk Shakes 29
57. Cappuccino Shake 29
58. Champagne Blood Shots 29
59. Champagne Party Punch 30
60. Cheery Cranberry Nog 30
61. Cherry Chip Shakes 31
62. Cherry Chocolate Floats 31
63. Cherry Cobbler Smoothies 32
64. Cherry Yogurt Smoothies 32
65. Cherry Berry Soy Smoothies 32
66. Chilled Lemon Coffees 33
67. Chilled Mocha Eggnog 33
68. Chocolate Banana Smoothies 34
69. Chocolate Coffee 34
70. Chocolate Malts 34
71. Chocolaty Banana Smoothie 35
72. Christmas Glow Punch 35
73. Cinnamon Apple Shakes 36
74. Citrus Cooler 36
75. Citrus Frost 36
76. Citrus Iced Tea 37
77. Citrus Iced Tea With Mint 37
78. Citrus Mint Cooler 37
79. Citrus Punch 38
80. Citrus Quencher 38
81. Citrus Tea Punch 39
82. Coffee Milk 39
83. Coffee Punch 39
84. Cola Floats 40
85. Cool Coffee Refresher 40
86. Cool Waters Shakes 40
87. Coquito 41
88. Cran Blueberry Smoothies 41

#	Title	Page
89.	Cran Raspberry Iced Tea	42
90.	Cranberry Beverage Syrup	42
91.	Cranberry Cooler	43
92.	Cranberry Orange Punch	43
93.	Cranberry Pomegranate Margaritas	43
94.	Cranberry Punch	44
95.	Cranberry Raspberry Punch	44
96.	Cranberry White Sangria	45
97.	Cranberry Banana Smoothies	45
98.	Cranberry Grape Spritzer	45
99.	Cranberry Jalapeno Martini	46
100.	Cransational Breakfast Drink	46
101.	Creamy Berry Shakes	47
102.	Creamy Berry Smoothies	47
103.	Creamy Holiday Eggnog	47
104.	Creamy Lime Coolers	48
105.	Creamy Mandarin Cooler	48
106.	Creamy Mocha Drink	49
107.	Creamy Orange Drink	49
108.	Creamy Orange Smoothies	50
109.	Creamy Strawberry Breeze	50
110.	Creamy Strawberry Punch	50
111.	Cucumber Melon Smoothies	51
112.	Diabetic Milk Shake	51
113.	Double Berry Smoothies	51
114.	Easy Lemon Lime Punch	52
115.	Effortless Eggnog	52
116.	Eggnog Shakes	53
117.	Festive Cranberry Drink	53
118.	Firecracker Mary	53
119.	Four Food Group Shakes	54
120.	Four Fruit Drink	54
121.	French Iced Coffee	55
122.	Fresh Lemonade Syrup	55
123.	Fresh Squeezed Pink Lemonade	55
124.	Frosty Chocolate Raspberry Latte	56
125.	Frosty Fruit Drink	56
126.	Frosty Fruit Slush	57
127.	Frosty Lemon Drink	57
128.	Frosty Mocha Drink	58
129.	Frosty Orange Smoothie	58
130.	Frosty's Fruit Slush	58
131.	Frothy Orange Drink	59
132.	Frothy Orange Pineapple Cooler	59
133.	Frozen Hot Chocolate	59
134.	Frozen Rhubarb Slush	60
135.	Frozen Strawberry Daiquiris	60
136.	Fruit Juice Cooler	61
137.	Fruit Punch	61
138.	Fruit Smoothies	61
139.	Fruited Punch	62
140.	Fruity Breakfast Beverage	62
141.	Fruity Lemonade	63
142.	Fruity Milk Shakes	63
143.	Fruity Mint Punch	63
144.	Fruity Punch	64
145.	Fruity Slush	64
146.	Fruity Summer Cooler	65
147.	Ginger Ale Fruit Punch	65
148.	Ginger Ale Mock Champagne	65
149.	Ginger Apple Fizz	66
150.	Ginger Peach Smoothies	66
151.	Ginger Kale Smoothies	66
152.	Golden Fruit Punch With Ice Ring	67
153.	Golden Smoothies	67
154.	Grape Juice Sparkler	68
155.	Grape Punch	68
156.	Grasshopper Shakes	68
157.	Grilled Lemon & Thyme Lemonade	69
158.	Grinch Punch	69
159.	Gummy Worm Punch	70
160.	Halloween Punch	70
161.	Herb Garden Tea	71
162.	Hibiscus Iced Tea	71
163.	Highbush Cranberry Tea	71
164.	Holiday Mimosa	72
165.	Homemade Holiday Eggnog	72
166.	Homemade Lemonade	72
167.	Homemade Limoncello	73
168.	Honey Berry Milk Shakes	73
169.	Honeydew Kiwi Cooler	74
170.	Honeydew Lime Cooler	74
171.	Hop, Skip And Go	74
172.	Horchata	75
173.	I'm A Little Teapot Tea	75
174.	Iced Coffee Latte	76
175.	Iced Coffee Slush	76
176.	Iced Honeydew Mint Tea	76
177.	Iced Lemon Tea	77
178.	Iced Melon Moroccan Mint Tea	77
179.	Iced Strawberry Tea	78
180.	Icy Holiday Punch	78
181.	Icy Lemonade	78
182.	Irish Creme Drink	79

#	Title	Page
183.	Irish Whiskey Float	79
184.	Kiwi Smoothies	80
185.	Lean Green Smoothie	80
186.	Lemon Berry Pitcher Punch	80
187.	Lemon Pineapple Smoothies	81
188.	Lemon Refresher	81
189.	Lemon Orange Iced Tea	81
190.	Leprechaun Lime Punch	82
191.	Lime Fizz	82
192.	Lime Milk Shakes	83
193.	Lime Milk Shakes For Two	83
194.	Lime Paradise	83
195.	Lime Sherbet Slush	84
196.	Limoncello Spritzer	84
197.	Long Island Iced Tea	84
198.	Lost In The Sun Punch	85
199.	Luscious Lime Slush	85
200.	Mad Scientist Punch	86
201.	Make Ahead Rhubarb Slush	86
202.	Makeover Nutty Monkey Malts	86
203.	Mango Lassi	87
204.	Mango Tango Smoothies	87
205.	Mango Green Tea Smoothies	87
206.	Martini	88
207.	Mint Tea Punch	88
208.	Minted Raspberry Lemonade	88
209.	Minty Orange Lemonade	89
210.	Mixed Berry Sangria	89
211.	Mocha Cappuccino Punch	90
212.	Mocha Cooler	90
213.	Mock Champagne Punch	90
214.	Mock Mint Julep	91
215.	Mock Strawberry Margaritas	91
216.	Mojito	92
217.	Morning Fruit Shake	92
218.	Nutty Banana Shakes	92
219.	Old Fashioned Chocolate Malted Milk	93
220.	Old Fashioned Eggnog	93
221.	Old Fashioned Ice Cream Soda	94
222.	Orange & Coffee Martini	94
223.	Orange Blueberry Shakes	94
224.	Orange Blush	95
225.	Orange Colada	95
226.	Orange Pineapple Punch	95
227.	Orange Pineapple Smoothies	96
228.	Orange Slush	96
229.	Orange Soy Milk Frappes	96
230.	Orange Strawberry Smoothies	97
231.	Orange Peach Thirst Quencher	97
232.	Paper Crafter's Punch	98
233.	Party Punch	98
234.	Peach Breakfast Slush	98
235.	Peach Smoothie	99
236.	Peach Smoothies	99
237.	Peach Wine Coolers	99
238.	Peachy Berry Shakes	100
239.	Peachy Buttermilk Shakes	100
240.	Peachy Lemonade	100
241.	Peachy Strawberry Smoothie	101
242.	Peanut Butter & Banana Smoothie	101
243.	Peanut Butter 'n' Jelly Breakfast Shake	102
244.	Pear Cooler	102
245.	Pear Slushy	102
246.	Pennsylvania Milk Punch	103
247.	Peppermint Eggnog Punch	103
248.	Picnic Fruit Punch	103
249.	Pineapple Cooler	104
250.	Pineapple Orange Slush	104
251.	Pineapple Punch	104
252.	Pineapple Sunrise Smoothies	105
253.	Pink Grapefruit Punch	105
254.	Pink Party Punch	106
255.	Pink Sparkling Wine Punch	106
256.	Poinsettia	107
257.	Pomegranate Champagne Cocktail	107
258.	Pomegranate Ginger Spritzer	107
259.	Pretty Pink Punch	108
260.	Pumpkin Patch Punch	108
261.	Purple Cows	109
262.	Purple People Eater Punch	109
263.	Quick Cranberry Fruit Punch	109
264.	Quick Watermelon Cooler	110
265.	Quick White Sangria	110
266.	Raindrop Raspberry Tea	110
267.	Raspberry Champagne Cocktail	111
268.	Raspberry Cream Smoothies	111
269.	Raspberry Mint Cooler	112
270.	Raspberry Pomegranate Smoothies	112
271.	Raspberry Refresher	112
272.	Raspberry Smoothies	113
273.	Raspberry Sweet Tea	113
274.	Red Carpet Tini	114
275.	Refreshing Citrus Iced Tea	114
276.	Refreshing Mojito	114

277. Rhubarb Cheesecake Smoothies 115
278. Rhubarb Punch 115
279. Rhubarb Slush 116
280. Rock A Bye Baby Punch 116
281. Rosy Rhubarb Punch 116
282. Sangria Wine 117
283. Santa's Orange Kissed Cocktail 117
284. Screwdriver 118
285. Sensational Slush 118
286. Sherbet Punch 118
287. Shrunken Apple Heads In Citrus Cider .. 119
288. Sidecar 119
289. Simple Citrus Punch 119
290. Simple Lemon Berry Pitcher Punch 120
291. Six Vegetable Juice 120
292. So Healthy Smoothies 121
293. Sour Mix 121
294. Sparkling Citrus Quencher 121
295. Sparkling Fruit Punch 122
296. Sparkling Peach Bellinis 122
297. Sparkling Pom Berry Splash 123
298. Sparkling Punch 123
299. Spiced Cider Punch 123
300. Spiced Green Tea 124
301. Spiced Iced Tea 124
302. Spiced Pineapple Cooler 124
303. Spicy Homemade Tomato Juice 125
304. Spring Strawberry Sangria 126
305. Starry Fruit Punch 126
306. Strawberry Banana Yogurt Shakes 126
307. Strawberry Banana Yogurt Smoothie 127
308. Strawberry Breakfast Shakes 127
309. Strawberry Cilantro Lemonade 128
310. Strawberry Citrus Slushies 128
311. Strawberry Cooler 129
312. Strawberry Flax Smoothies 129
313. Strawberry Lemonade Slush 129
314. Strawberry Lime Smoothies 130
315. Strawberry Mango Smoothies For 2 130
316. Strawberry Melon Fizz 131
317. Strawberry Party Punch 131
318. Strawberry Peach Banana Smoothie 131
319. Strawberry Pineapple Punch 132
320. Strawberry Shakes 132
321. Strawberry Smoothie 132
322. Strawberry Yogurt Smoothies 133
323. Strawberry Carrot Smoothies 133
324. Strawberry Peach Milk Shakes 134
325. Sugar Free Holiday Nog 134
326. Summertime Fruit Tea 134
327. Summertime Tea 135
328. Sun Kissed Smoothies 135
329. Sunny Orange Lemonade 136
330. Sunny Slush 136
331. Sunrise Sipper 136
332. Sunrise Slushies 137
333. Super Mango Smoothies 137
334. Sweet Citrus Iced Tea 137
335. Sweet Citrus Punch 138
336. Sweet Raspberry Tea 138
337. Sweet Tea Concentrate 139
338. Tangy Fruit Punch 139
339. Tangy Party Punch 140
340. Tangy Strawberry Slush 140
341. Tequila Sunrise 140
342. Thick Peachy Milk Shakes 141
343. Thirst Quenching Limeade 141
344. Three Fruit Slushies 142
345. Three Fruit Smoothies 142
346. Tipsy Iced Coffee 142
347. Triple Berry Smoothies 143
348. Tropical Fruit Punch 143
349. Tropical Fruit Slush 144
350. Tropical Fruit Smoothies 144
351. Tropical Lime Punch 145
352. Tropical Lime Smoothies 145
353. Tropical Punch 145
354. Vampire Killer 146
355. Watermelon Cooler 146
356. Watermelon Slush 146
357. Watermelon Spritzer 147
358. Whipped Banana Latte 147
359. Whiskey Sour 147
360. White Christmas Sangria 148
361. White Grape Punch 148
362. Wisconsin Whammer 148
363. Witches' Brew 149
364. Yogurt Breakfast Drink 149
365. Yogurt Fruit Smoothies 150

INDEX 151

CONCLUSION 153

365 Awesome Cold Beverage Recipes

***

1. Almond Lemonade Tea

Serving: 16 servings (4 quarts) | Prep: 10mins | Cook: 0mins | Ready in:

Ingredients

- 1 can (12 ounces) frozen lemonade concentrate, thawed
- 1 cup sugar
- 3 to 4 tablespoons unsweetened instant tea
- 1 tablespoon almond extract
- 1 tablespoon vanilla extract
- 14 cups water

Direction

- Combine the initial 5 ingredients in a 1-gallon container and mix well. Pour in 8 cups of water and stir till blended. Add the leftover water then serve over ice.

Nutrition Information

- Calories: 94 calories
- Sodium: 2mg sodium
- Fiber: 0 fiber)
- Total Carbohydrate: 23g carbohydrate (21g sugars
- Cholesterol: 0 cholesterol
- Protein: 0 protein.
- Total Fat: 0 fat (0 saturated fat)

2. American Beauty

Serving: Serves 1. | Prep: | Cook: |Ready in:

Ingredients

- 1 ounce brandy
- 1/2 ounce dry vermouth
- 1/4 teaspoon white crème de menthe
- 1 ounce orange juice
- 1 teaspoon grenadine
- 1 ounce tawny port
- 3 or 4 ice cubes

Direction

- In a cocktail shaker, combine grenadine, orange juice, crème de menthe, vermouth and brandy then shake vigorously. In a cocktail glass, strain the drink then let a port float on top.

3. Apple Brandy

Serving: 2 quarts. | Prep: 35mins | Cook: 0mins |Ready in:

Ingredients

- 4 cups sugar
- 2 cups water
- 4 pounds apples, sliced
- 1 liter brandy
- 3 whole cloves
- 1 cinnamon stick (3 inches)
- Additional whole cloves and cinnamon sticks

Direction

- In a large saucepan, combine water and sugar then boil. Cook and stir to dissolve the sugar. Take away from the heat.
- In a plastic container or a large glass, place apples then add cinnamon sticks, cloves,

- brandy and sugar mixture. Allow to stand for at least 2 weeks at room temperature with a cover, stir once per week.
- Strain the brandy mixture then remove spices and apples. Transfer into glass bottles. Add 1 cinnamon stick and an additional 3 cloves into each bottle.

Nutrition Information

- Calories: 123 calories
- Fiber: 0 fiber)
- Total Carbohydrate: 19g carbohydrate (19g sugars
- Cholesterol: 0 cholesterol
- Protein: 0 protein.
- Total Fat: 0 fat (0 saturated fat)
- Sodium: 0 sodium

4. Apple Cider Sipper

Serving: 1 serving. | Prep: 5mins | Cook: 0mins | Ready in:

Ingredients

- Red-colored sugar
- Grenadine syrup
- 4 ounces chilled apple cider or juice
- 2 ounces apple schnapps liqueur
- 2 drops green food coloring

Direction

- On a plate, sprinkle a thin layer of sugar. Using grenadine syrup, dampen the rim of a martini glass then dip rim in the plate of sugar. Pour in apple juice to the glass; gently stir in food coloring and liqueur.

Nutrition Information

- Calories:
- Sodium:
- Fiber:
- Total Carbohydrate:
- Cholesterol:
- Protein:
- Total Fat:

5. Apple Grape Drink

Serving: 3-3/4 quarts. | Prep: 15mins | Cook: 0mins | Ready in:

Ingredients

- 6 cups apple juice, chilled
- 3 cups white grape juice, chilled
- 1 can (12 ounces) frozen lemonade concentrate, thawed
- 1 liter club soda, chilled

Direction

- Mix lemonade concentrate and juices in a big container. Whisk in club soda and transfer into cold glasses. Serve promptly.

Nutrition Information

- Calories: 117 calories
- Total Carbohydrate: 29g carbohydrate (27g sugars
- Cholesterol: 0 cholesterol
- Protein: 0 protein.
- Total Fat: 0 fat (0 saturated fat)
- Sodium: 21mg sodium
- Fiber: 0 fiber)

6. Apple Martini

Serving: 1 | Prep: 5mins | Cook: | Ready in:

Ingredients

- 1 (1.5 fluid ounce) jigger best-quality vodka
- 1 (1.5 fluid ounce) jigger apple schnapps
- 1 (1.5 fluid ounce) jigger frozen lemonade
- 1 (1.5 fluid ounce) jigger chilled lemon-lime soda
- 1 lime wedge
- 1 maraschino cherries

Direction

- Pour soda, lemonade, schnapps and vodka over ice in a cocktail shaker. Cover and shake till it's frosty on the outside of the shaker. Into a chilled martini glass, strain the drink. Use maraschino cherry and lime wedge to garnish. Serve.

7. Apple Pie In A Glass

Serving: 2 servings. | Prep: 5mins | Cook: 0mins | Ready in:

Ingredients

- 1/2 cup fat-free milk
- 1 cup low-fat vanilla frozen yogurt
- 1/2 cup apple pie filling
- 1/4 teaspoon ground cinnamon

Direction

- Combine all the ingredients in a blender and cover it. Process the mixture until smooth. Pour it into the glasses to serve.

Nutrition Information

- Calories: 189 calories
- Sodium: 120mg sodium
- Fiber: 1g fiber)
- Total Carbohydrate: 39g carbohydrate (0 sugars
- Cholesterol: 6mg cholesterol
- Protein: 7g protein. Diabetic Exchanges: 1-1/2 fruit
- Total Fat: 1g fat (1g saturated fat)

8. Apricot Brandy Slush

Serving: 20 | Prep: 10mins | Cook: 15mins | Ready in:

Ingredients

- 9 cups water, divided
- 3 cups white sugar
- 2 tea bags
- 1 (12 fluid ounce) can frozen orange juice
- 1 (12 fluid ounce) can frozen lemonade
- 16 fluid ounces apricot brandy

Direction

- In a large saucepan, boil 7 cups of water. Stir in sugar for 5 minutes till dissolved. Take away from the heat and cool syrup for 30 minutes to room temperature.
- In a small saucepan, boil 2 cups of water. Take away from the heat and place in tea bags. Let steep for 30 minutes till the water reaches room temperature. Remove then discard tea bags.
- Pour over syrup with brewed tea. Stir in apricot brandy, lemonade and orange juice till well combined. Transfer into a container with wide mouth. Store the slush mixture for 3 days in the freezer; use a wooden spoon to stir 2 times per day to get a slushy consistency.

Nutrition Information

- Calories: 247 calories;
- Total Carbohydrate: 46.7
- Cholesterol: 0
- Protein: 0.5
- Total Fat: 0.1
- Sodium: 5

9. Apricot Peach Smoothies

Serving: 4 servings. | Prep: 10mins | Cook: 0mins | Ready in:

Ingredients

- 1 can (5-1/2 ounces) apricot nectar
- 1 medium ripe banana, frozen and cut into chunks
- 1 cup fat-free vanilla yogurt
- 2 cups sliced fresh or frozen unsweetened peaches
- 1 tablespoon lemon juice
- 1 tablespoon honey
- 1 teaspoon grated lemon zest
- 6 ice cubes

Direction

- Combine all of the ingredients in a food processor or a blender. Cover then blend till smooth. Transfer into chilled glasses and serve at once.

Nutrition Information

- Calories: 160 calories
- Protein: 4g protein.
- Total Fat: 0 fat (0 saturated fat)
- Sodium: 35mg sodium
- Fiber: 3g fiber)
- Total Carbohydrate: 37g carbohydrate (0 sugars
- Cholesterol: 2mg cholesterol

10. Baby Shower Punch

Serving: 3-1/2 quarts. | Prep: 15mins | Cook: 5mins | Ready in:

Ingredients

- 8 cups chopped fresh or frozen rhubarb, thawed (about 2 pounds)
- 6 cups water
- 3-1/2 cups grapefruit juice
- 2-1/2 cups sugar
- 1/4 cup lemon juice
- 1 liter ginger ale, chilled

Direction

- Boil water and rhubarb in a large saucepan. Lower heat then let simmer for 10-12 minutes, uncovered, till rhubarb is very tender. Strain and remove pulp. Bring the rhubarb juice back to the saucepan. Pour in lemon juice, sugar and grapefruit juice. Boil then cook and stir to dissolve the sugar. Let cool slightly then store in the fridge, covered, to chill. Place into a punch bowl then add in ginger ale and stir right before serving.

Nutrition Information

- Calories: 201 calories
- Protein: 1g protein.
- Total Fat: 0 fat (0 saturated fat)
- Sodium: 9mg sodium
- Fiber: 1g fiber)
- Total Carbohydrate: 51g carbohydrate (48g sugars
- Cholesterol: 0 cholesterol

11. Banana Breakfast Smoothies

Serving: 2 servings. | Prep: 10mins | Cook: 0mins | Ready in:

Ingredients

- 1 cup fat-free milk
- 1/2 cup fat-free plain yogurt
- 1/4 cup toasted wheat germ
- 2 small ripe bananas, sliced and frozen
- 1 teaspoon sugar
- 1 teaspoon vanilla extract
- Ground nutmeg

Direction

- In a blender, add the first six ingredients. Cover and blend until smooth, about 1 to 2 minutes. Transfer into cold glasses then sprinkle with nutmeg. Serve promptly.

Nutrition Information

- Calories: 221 calories
- Sodium: 99mg sodium
- Fiber: 4g fiber)
- Total Carbohydrate: 43g carbohydrate (30g sugars
- Cholesterol: 4mg cholesterol
- Protein: 12g protein.
- Total Fat: 2g fat (1g saturated fat)

12. Banana Cocoa Smoothies

Serving: 3 servings. | Prep: 10mins | Cook: 0mins | Ready in:

Ingredients

- 1 cup (8 ounces) fat-free vanilla yogurt
- 3/4 cup fat-free milk
- 1 medium ripe banana, frozen and cut into chunks
- 3 tablespoons sugar-free chocolate drink mix
- 1/4 teaspoon vanilla extract

Direction

- Mix all ingredients in a blender. Blend until smooth, covered, then transfer into cold glasses. Serve promptly.

Nutrition Information

- Calories: 155 calories
- Total Fat: 1g fat (0 saturated fat)
- Sodium: 100mg sodium
- Fiber: 2g fiber)
- Total Carbohydrate: 30g carbohydrate (0 sugars
- Cholesterol: 3mg cholesterol
- Protein: 7g protein. Diabetic Exchanges: 1 fruit

13. Banana Coffee Smoothie

Serving: 1 serving. | Prep: 10mins | Cook: 0mins | Ready in:

Ingredients

- 3/4 cup 2% milk
- 1/3 cup coffee yogurt
- 1 small banana, frozen, peeled and cut into chunks
- 1/8 teaspoon ground cinnamon
- Dash ground nutmeg

Direction

- Mix all ingredients in a blender. Cover and blend until blended, for 45 to 60 seconds. Transfer into a cold glass and serve promptly.

Nutrition Information

- Calories: 266 calories
- Cholesterol: 18mg cholesterol
- Protein: 10g protein.
- Total Fat: 5g fat (3g saturated fat)
- Sodium: 136mg sodium
- Fiber: 3g fiber)
- Total Carbohydrate: 48g carbohydrate (43g sugars

14. Banana Milk Drink

Serving: 2 servings. | Prep: 5mins | Cook: 0mins | Ready in:

Ingredients

- 1 large ripe banana
- 1 cup milk
- 1-1/2 to 2 teaspoons sugar
- 1/2 teaspoon vanilla extract
- Dash ground cinnamon, optional

Direction

- In a blender, add the first four ingredients then cover and blend until smooth. Transfer into glasses and if you want, sprinkle with cinnamon. Serve promptly.

Nutrition Information

- Calories: 120 calories
- Protein: 5g protein. Diabetic Exchanges: 1-1/2 fruit
- Total Fat: 0 fat (0 saturated fat)
- Sodium: 66mg sodium
- Fiber: 2g fiber)
- Total Carbohydrate: 26g carbohydrate (0 sugars
- Cholesterol: 3mg cholesterol

15. Banana Mixed Berry Smoothie

Serving: 3 servings. | Prep: 5mins | Cook: 0mins | Ready in:

Ingredients

- 1 cup vanilla yogurt
- 1 medium ripe banana, peeled, cut into chunks and frozen
- 1/4 cup each frozen unsweetened strawberries, blueberries, raspberries and blackberries
- 1 cup milk

Direction

- Mix all ingredients in a food processor or a blender. Cover and blend until smooth, then transfer into cold glasses and serve promptly.

Nutrition Information

- Calories: 192 calories
- Sodium: 94mg sodium
- Fiber: 2g fiber)
- Total Carbohydrate: 30g carbohydrate (26g sugars
- Cholesterol: 19mg cholesterol
- Protein: 7g protein.
- Total Fat: 6g fat (3g saturated fat)

16. Banana Nog

Serving: 11 servings (about 2 quarts). | Prep: 5mins | Cook: 15mins | Ready in:

Ingredients

- 3 cups milk, divided
- 3 cups half-and-half cream, divided
- 3 egg yolks
- 3/4 cup sugar
- 3 large ripe bananas
- 1/2 cup light rum
- 1/3 cup creme de cacao
- 1-1/2 teaspoons vanilla extract
- Whipped cream and baking cocoa, optional

Direction

- Mix 1-1/2 cups cream, 1-1/2 cups milk, sugar and egg yolks together in a big and heavy saucepan. Over medium-low heat stir the mixture until it is 160°F and it achieves a thick consistency that can coat the back of a spoon.
- Blend bananas in a food processor. In a pitcher, put milk mixture and mix in the blended bananas, crème de cacao, vanilla, rum, remaining milk and cream. Cover the pitcher and place in the fridge for at least 3 hours serve once chilled.
- Put in chilled glasses. Finish off with whipped cream and a pinch of cocoa on top if you want.

Nutrition Information

- Calories: 282 calories
- Fiber: 1g fiber)
- Total Carbohydrate: 31g carbohydrate (27g sugars
- Cholesterol: 95mg cholesterol
- Protein: 5g protein.
- Total Fat: 10g fat (6g saturated fat)
- Sodium: 62mg sodium

17. Banana Pineapple Slush

Serving: about 9-1/2 quarts. | Prep: 10mins | Cook: 0mins | Ready in:

Ingredients

- 4 cups sugar
- 2 cups water
- 1 can (46 ounces) pineapple juice
- 3 cups orange juice
- 3/4 cup lemon juice
- 1/2 cup orange juice concentrate
- 8 medium ripe bananas, mashed
- 2 bottles (2 liters each) cream soda
- 3 cans (12 ounces each) lemon-lime soda

Direction

- Bring water and sugar in a saucepan to a boil on medium heat then allow to cool. Transfer into a freezer container. Put in bananas, orange juice concentrate and juices. Cover and freeze the mixture. When ready to serve, thaw mixture until slushy and whisk in lemon-lime soda and cream soda.

Nutrition Information

- Calories: 119 calories
- Total Fat: 0 fat (0 saturated fat)
- Sodium: 23mg sodium
- Fiber: 1g fiber)
- Total Carbohydrate: 30g carbohydrate (0 sugars
- Cholesterol: 0 cholesterol
- Protein: 0 protein. Diabetic Exchanges: 2 fruit.

18. Banana Split Smoothies

Serving: 4 servings. | Prep: 15mins | Cook: 0mins | Ready in:

Ingredients

- 2 medium ripe bananas
- 1 can (8 ounces) crushed pineapple, drained
- 1-1/2 cups milk
- 1/2 cup fresh or frozen unsweetened sliced strawberries
- 2 tablespoons honey
- 5 ice cubes
- Whipped topping, chocolate syrup and maraschino cherries

Direction

- Mix together the first 5 ingredients in a blender; process with a cover till smooth. Slowly include ice, blending till slushy. Transfer into chilled glasses. Garnish with cherries, chocolate syrup and whipped topping. Serve immediately.

Nutrition Information

- Calories: 183 calories
- Total Fat: 3g fat (2g saturated fat)
- Sodium: 47mg sodium
- Fiber: 2g fiber)
- Total Carbohydrate: 37g carbohydrate (32g sugars
- Cholesterol: 12mg cholesterol
- Protein: 4g protein.

19. Banana Strawberry Smoothies

Serving: 2 servings. | Prep: 15mins | Cook: 0mins | Ready in:

Ingredients

- 1-1/2 cups vanilla or plain yogurt
- 2/3 cup orange juice
- 2 medium ripe bananas, cut into chunks
- 1 cup halved fresh strawberries
- 2 teaspoons honey

Direction

- Mix all ingredients in a blender, then cover and blend until smooth. Transfer into cold glasses and serve promptly.

Nutrition Information

- Calories: 375 calories
- Sodium: 121mg sodium
- Fiber: 5g fiber)
- Total Carbohydrate: 72g carbohydrate (63g sugars
- Cholesterol: 18mg cholesterol
- Protein: 11g protein.
- Total Fat: 7g fat (4g saturated fat)

20. Banana And Chocolate Smoothie

Serving: 4 servings. | Prep: 10mins | Cook: 0mins | Ready in:

Ingredients

- 1 cup milk
- 1 cup vanilla yogurt
- 1/2 cup chocolate syrup
- 2 medium bananas, halved
- 8 ice cubes

Direction

- Mix all ingredients in a blender then cover and blend until smooth. Turn into cold glasses and serve promptly.

Nutrition Information

- Calories: 256 calories
- Sodium: 89mg sodium
- Fiber: 2g fiber)
- Total Carbohydrate: 49g carbohydrate (43g sugars
- Cholesterol: 14mg cholesterol
- Protein: 6g protein.
- Total Fat: 5g fat (3g saturated fat)

21. Banana Almond Milk Shakes

Serving: 4 servings. | Prep: 10mins | Cook: 0mins | Ready in:

Ingredients

- 1-1/4 cups unsweetened almond milk
- 6 frozen medium ripe bananas, cut into chunks
- 1/4 cup almond butter
- 1/2 teaspoon vanilla extract
- 1/4 teaspoon almond extract
- 1/3 cup semisweet chocolate chips
- Sweetened whipped cream, optional

Direction

- Combine the five ingredients in a blender. Cover and process it for 2 minutes or until smooth. Add the chocolate chips and cover and process it again for 30 more seconds or until well-blended.
- Pour the drink into the chilled glasses. If desired, garnish it with whipped cream. Serve.

Nutrition Information

- Calories: 342 calories

- Total Carbohydrate: 55g carbohydrate (33g sugars
- Cholesterol: 0 cholesterol
- Protein: 6g protein.
- Total Fat: 14g fat (4g saturated fat)
- Sodium: 89mg sodium
- Fiber: 7g fiber)

22. Basil Citrus Cocktail

Serving: 1 serving. | Prep: 10mins | Cook: 0mins |Ready in:

Ingredients

- 6 fresh basil leaves
- 1-1/2 to 2 cups ice cubes
- 2 ounces white grapefruit juice
- 2 ounces mandarin orange juice
- 3/4 ounce gin
- 1/2 ounce Domaine de Canton ginger liqueur

Direction

- Muddle basil leaves in a shaker.
- Add ice to fill 3/4 of a shaker. Pour in ginger liqueur, gin and juice. Cover then shake till it forms condensation on the outside of the shaker, for 10-15 seconds. In a chilled cocktail glass, drain the drink.

Nutrition Information

- Calories: 136 calories
- Cholesterol: 0 cholesterol
- Protein: 1g protein.
- Total Fat: 0 fat (0 saturated fat)
- Sodium: 0 sodium
- Fiber: 0 fiber)
- Total Carbohydrate: 14g carbohydrate (7g sugars

23. Basil Tomato Juice

Serving: about 2-1/2 quarts. | Prep: 20mins | Cook: 55mins |Ready in:

Ingredients

- 8 pounds ripe tomatoes, quartered
- 2 celery ribs, chopped
- 1 medium onion, chopped
- 1/4 cup finely chopped fresh basil
- 1/4 cup lemon juice
- 2 tablespoons sugar
- 1 tablespoon Worcestershire sauce
- 1 teaspoon salt
- 3/4 teaspoon hot pepper sauce

Direction

- Combine onion, celery and tomatoes in a stock pot the boil. Lower heat and let simmer, uncovered, while stirring occasionally till tender, for 45 minutes.
- Let the tomato mixture cool slightly then put through a food mill or a sieve. Bring back to the pan. Add in the leftover ingredients and stir. Boil then take away from the heat and let cool. Pour into a pitcher then store in the fridge, covered, to chill.

Nutrition Information

- Calories: 66 calories
- Protein: 3g protein. Diabetic Exchanges: 2 vegetable.
- Total Fat: 1g fat (0 saturated fat)
- Sodium: 215mg sodium
- Fiber: 4g fiber)
- Total Carbohydrate: 15g carbohydrate (10g sugars
- Cholesterol: 0 cholesterol

24. Beer Margaritas

Serving: 6 | Prep: 5mins | Cook: | Ready in:

Ingredients

- 1 (12 fluid ounce) can frozen limeade concentrate
- 12 fluid ounces tequila
- 12 fluid ounces water
- 12 fluid ounces beer
- ice
- 1 lime, cut into wedges

Direction

- In a big pitcher, mix beer, limeade, water, and tequila together until the limeade melts and the mixture is well combined. Put a lot of ice then add lime wedges to garnish. If necessary, pour in more water.

25. Bella Basil Raspberry Tea

Serving: 6 servings. | Prep: 35mins | Cook: 10mins | Ready in:

Ingredients

- 3 cups fresh raspberries
- 1 cup sugar
- 1 cup packed fresh basil leaves, coarsely chopped
- 1/4 cup lime juice
- 2 individual black tea bags
- 1 bottle (1 liter) carbonated water or 1 bottle (750 milliliters) sparkling rose wine
- Ice cubes
- Fresh raspberries, optional

Direction

- Combine lime juice, basil, sugar and raspberries in a large saucepan. Mash the berries then cook till they release juices over medium heat, about 7 minutes.
- Take away from the heat and place in tea bags. Steep, covered, for 20 minutes. Strain the mixture, removing raspberry seeds and tea bags. Pour tea into a 2-quart pitcher. Store in the fridge, covered, till serving.
- Gradually add wine or carbonated water right before serving. Pour over ice to serve. Place raspberries on top if preferred.

Nutrition Information

- Calories: 281 calories
- Protein: 1g protein.
- Total Fat: 0 fat (0 saturated fat)
- Sodium: 9mg sodium
- Fiber: 4g fiber)
- Total Carbohydrate: 44g carbohydrate (37g sugars
- Cholesterol: 0 cholesterol

26. Berry Banana Smoothies

Serving: 3 servings. | Prep: 10mins | Cook: 0mins | Ready in:

Ingredients

- 1 cup vanilla yogurt
- 1 medium ripe banana, peeled, cut into chunks and frozen
- 1/4 cup each frozen unsweetened strawberries, blueberries, raspberries and blackberries
- 1 cup fat-free milk

Direction

- Mix all ingredients in a blender, then cover and blend until smooth. Transfer into cold glasses and serve promptly.

Nutrition Information

- Calories: 161 calories

- Total Fat: 1g fat (1g saturated fat)
- Sodium: 98mg sodium
- Fiber: 2g fiber)
- Total Carbohydrate: 31g carbohydrate (0 sugars
- Cholesterol: 6mg cholesterol
- Protein: 8g protein. Diabetic Exchanges: 1 fruit

27. Berry Breakfast Smoothies

Serving: 5 servings. | Prep: 5mins | Cook: 0mins | Ready in:

Ingredients

- 2 cups cranberry juice
- 2 containers (6 ounces each) raspberry yogurt
- 1 cup frozen unsweetened raspberries
- 1 cup frozen unsweetened blueberries
- 8 ice cubes

Direction

- Mix all ingredients in a blender, then cover and blend until combined, about 30-45 seconds. Transfer into cold glasses and serve promptly.

Nutrition Information

- Calories: 141 calories
- Total Fat: 1g fat (1g saturated fat)
- Sodium: 39mg sodium
- Fiber: 2g fiber)
- Total Carbohydrate: 31g carbohydrate (29g sugars
- Cholesterol: 3mg cholesterol
- Protein: 4g protein.

28. Berry Delicious Smoothies

Serving: 4 servings. | Prep: 10mins | Cook: 0mins | Ready in:

Ingredients

- 1-1/2 cups fat-free strawberry Greek yogurt
- 3/4 cup acai mixed berry V8 juice blend
- 1 cup frozen unsweetened strawberries
- 1 cup frozen unsweetened blueberries
- 1/2 cup frozen unsweetened raspberries
- 1/2 cup frozen unsweetened blackberries
- 1/2 cup frozen pitted dark sweet cherries
- 1/4 cup wheat bran
- 1 teaspoon ground flaxseed

Direction

- Mix all ingredients in a blender, then cover and blend until smooth, or for half a minute. Transfer into cold glasses and serve promptly.

Nutrition Information

- Calories: 167 calories
- Total Fat: 1g fat (0 saturated fat)
- Sodium: 47mg sodium
- Fiber: 6g fiber)
- Total Carbohydrate: 33g carbohydrate (26g sugars
- Cholesterol: 0 cholesterol
- Protein: 9g protein. Diabetic Exchanges: 1 starch

29. Berry Fruity Punch

Serving: 11 cups. | Prep: 15mins | Cook: 0mins | Ready in:

Ingredients

- 2 cups unsweetened pineapple juice
- 2 cups fresh or frozen unsweetened raspberries

- 2 cups fresh strawberries
- 2 cups cubed honeydew
- 1 cup cubed seedless watermelon
- 3/4 cup sugar
- 1/2 teaspoon ground ginger
- 4 cups diet ginger ale, chilled
- 1 cup lime juice, chilled
- 1/2 cup lemon juice, chilled

Direction

- Process batches of melon, berries and pineapple juice in a blender.
- In a large pitcher or a punch bowl, strain and place the fruit mixture. Add ginger and sugar; stir. Pour in lemon juice, lime juice and ginger ale. In chilled glasses, pour over crushed ice just before serving.

Nutrition Information

- Calories: 121 calories
- Fiber: 3g fiber)
- Total Carbohydrate: 31g carbohydrate (0 sugars
- Cholesterol: 0 cholesterol
- Protein: 1g protein. Diabetic Exchanges: 2 fruit.
- Total Fat: 0 fat (0 saturated fat)
- Sodium: 27mg sodium

30. Berry Nutritious Smoothies

Serving: 3 servings. | Prep: 5mins | Cook: 0mins | Ready in:

Ingredients

- 1 cup orange juice
- 1/2 cup fat-free plain yogurt
- 1/2 cup silken firm tofu
- 1 medium ripe banana, sliced and frozen
- 1/2 cup frozen unsweetened strawberries
- 1/2 cup frozen unsweetened raspberries
- 2 tablespoons toasted wheat germ

Direction

- Mix whole ingredients in a blender, then cover and blend until smooth, about a half minute. Transfer into cold glasses and serve promptly.

Nutrition Information

- Calories: 141 calories
- Cholesterol: 1mg cholesterol
- Protein: 6g protein.
- Total Fat: 1g fat (0 saturated fat)
- Sodium: 35mg sodium
- Fiber: 3g fiber)
- Total Carbohydrate: 28g carbohydrate (17g sugars

31. Berry Slush

Serving: 5 quarts. | Prep: 10mins | Cook: 0mins | Ready in:

Ingredients

- 1 package (3 ounces) berry blue or raspberry gelatin
- 2 cups boiling water
- 2 cups sugar
- 1 can (46 ounces) pineapple juice
- 2 liters ginger ale
- 4-1/2 cups cold water
- 1 cup lemon juice
- Blue or red liquid food coloring, optional
- Fresh raspberries, blueberries and star fruit, optional

Direction

- Dissolve gelatin in a big container filled with boiling water. Whisk in sugar until dissolved. Put in lemon juice, water, ginger ale and pineapple juice. Put in food coloring, if

wanted. Place in the freezer about 8 hours or overnight.
- Before serving, take out of the freezer about 20 minutes. Whisk the mixture until slushy. Serve in a cold glass, thread fruit on wooden skewers to decorate, if wanted. Serve promptly.

Nutrition Information

- Calories: 167 calories
- Protein: 1g protein.
- Total Fat: 0 fat (0 saturated fat)
- Sodium: 18mg sodium
- Fiber: 0 fiber)
- Total Carbohydrate: 43g carbohydrate (41g sugars
- Cholesterol: 0 cholesterol

32. Berry Smoothie

Serving: | Prep: | Cook: | Ready in:

Ingredients

- 1 cup Orange Juice
- 1 cup Yogurt (or sub avocado for dairy free)
- 1 cup Spinach
- 1 Banana
- 2 cups Berries, frozen unsweetened
- 1 tablespoon Chia Seeds (optional)

Direction

- Add ingredients in the order listed with liquid first and frozen on top.
- Blend until smooth.

33. Berry Smoothies

Serving: 2 | Prep: | Cook: | Ready in:

Ingredients

- 2 cups mixed frozen berries
- 1 (6 ounce) container blueberry fat-free yogurt
- ½ cup light cranberry-raspberry juice
- ⅓ cup nonfat dry milk powder
- 1 tablespoon fresh blueberries (optional)

Direction

- Mix together dry milk powder, juice, yogurt and frozen berries in a blender. Cover and process until smooth, then transfer into 2 glasses. Decorate with fresh blueberries if you want.

Nutrition Information

- Calories: 164 calories;
- Total Fat: 0
- Cholesterol: 4
- Total Carbohydrate: 32
- Sugar: 14
- Saturated Fat: 0
- Sodium: 130
- Fiber: 5
- Protein: 9

34. Berry Splash Smoothies

Serving: 3 servings. | Prep: 10mins | Cook: 0mins | Ready in:

Ingredients

- 1/4 cup fat-free milk
- 1 cup (8 ounces) cherry yogurt
- 2 cups frozen unsweetened mixed berries
- 1/4 cup fresh blueberries, divided
- Sugar, optional
- 3 tablespoons vanilla yogurt

Direction

- Mix together half of the blueberries, mixed berries, cherry yogurt, milk and sugar (if you want) in a blender, then cover and blend until smooth. If needed, give it a stir. Transfer into cold glasses and put on top with vanilla yogurt, then sprinkle with the leftover blueberries.

Nutrition Information

- Calories: 157 calories
- Cholesterol: 6mg cholesterol
- Protein: 5g protein.
- Total Fat: 1g fat (1g saturated fat)
- Sodium: 59mg sodium
- Fiber: 2g fiber)
- Total Carbohydrate: 32g carbohydrate (27g sugars

35. Berry Yogurt Shakes

Serving: 4 servings. | Prep: 5mins | Cook: 0mins | Ready in:

Ingredients

- 2 cups (16 ounces) lemon yogurt
- 1-1/2 cups fat-free milk
- 1 cup unsweetened raspberries
- Sugar substitute equivalent to 2 tablespoons sugar

Direction

- Combine all of the ingredients in a blender. Cover the blender and process the mixture until smooth. Pour it into the chilled glasses and serve.

Nutrition Information

- Calories: 152 calories
- Sodium: 161mg sodium
- Fiber: 2g fiber)
- Total Carbohydrate: 25g carbohydrate (0 sugars
- Cholesterol: 7mg cholesterol
- Protein: 9g protein. Diabetic Exchanges: 1 starch
- Total Fat: 2g fat (1g saturated fat)

36. Black Eyed Susan

Serving: 1 serving. | Prep: 5mins | Cook: 0mins | Ready in:

Ingredients

- 1/2 to 3/4 cup crushed ice
- 1 ounce vodka
- 1 ounce light rum
- 1/2 ounce Triple Sec
- 2 ounces unsweetened pineapple juice
- 2 ounces orange juice
- Lime slice and pitted sweet dark cherry

Direction

- In a rocks glass, place the desired amount of ice then add juices, Triple Sec, rum and vodka. Stir then add cherry and a slice of lime to serve.

Nutrition Information

- Calories: 242 calories
- Sodium: 3mg sodium
- Fiber: 0 fiber)
- Total Carbohydrate: 21g carbohydrate (18g sugars
- Cholesterol: 0 cholesterol
- Protein: 0 protein.
- Total Fat: 0 fat (0 saturated fat)

37. Blackberry Banana Smoothies

Serving: 4 servings. | Prep: 15mins | Cook: 0mins | Ready in:

Ingredients

- 2 cups orange juice
- 1/3 cup vanilla yogurt
- 2 medium ripe bananas, cut into thirds and frozen
- 1/2 cup fresh or frozen blackberries

Direction

- Mix all ingredients in a blender. Cover and blend until well combined. Transfer into cold glass and serve promptly.

Nutrition Information

- Calories: 136 calories
- Protein: 2g protein. Diabetic Exchanges: 1 starch
- Total Fat: 1g fat (1g saturated fat)
- Sodium: 14mg sodium
- Fiber: 2g fiber)
- Total Carbohydrate: 32g carbohydrate (0 sugars
- Cholesterol: 1mg cholesterol

38. Blackberry Brandy Slush

Serving: 28 servings (1 cup each). | Prep: 10mins | Cook: 0mins | Ready in:

Ingredients

- 8 cups water
- 2 cups sugar
- 3 cups blackberry brandy
- 1 can (12 ounces) frozen lemonade concentrate, thawed
- 1 can (12 ounces) frozen grape juice concentrate, thawed
- 14 cups lemon-lime soda, chilled

Direction

- Stir sugar and water together in a big bowl until sugar has dissolved. Stir in juice concentrates and brandy. Turn to freezer containers and put in the freezer overnight.
- In each glass, add 1/2 cup brandy mixture then pour 1/2 cup soda on top to serve.

Nutrition Information

- Calories: 235 calories
- Fiber: 0 fiber)
- Total Carbohydrate: 51g carbohydrate (48g sugars
- Cholesterol: 0 cholesterol
- Protein: 0 protein.
- Total Fat: 0 fat (0 saturated fat)
- Sodium: 18mg sodium

39. Blackberry Lemonade

Serving: 4 | Prep: 10mins | Cook: | Ready in:

Ingredients

- 3 tablespoons blackberries
- 1 1/3 cups boiling water
- 1/2 cup white sugar
- 5 lemons, juiced
- 3 1/2 cups water
- ice cubes

Direction

- Put blackberries into a bowl. Add on top with boiling water. Allow it to sit for 10 minutes until steam ceases to rise from the bowl.
- Turn the mixture into a pitcher and stir in sugar. Add in cold water and lemon juice. Put it in the fridge until refrigerated. Serve over ice cubes.

Nutrition Information

- Calories: 102 calories;
- Total Fat: 0.1
- Sodium: 11
- Total Carbohydrate: 26.1
- Cholesterol: 0
- Protein: 0.2

40. Blended Fruit Chiller

Serving: 6 servings. | Prep: 10mins | Cook: 0mins | Ready in:

Ingredients

- 3 cups (24 ounces) fat-free plain yogurt
- 1 cup unsweetened pineapple juice, chilled
- 1 cup fresh or frozen unsweetened strawberries
- 1 medium ripe banana, sliced
- 1/2 cup fresh or canned unsweetened pineapple chunks
- 3 tablespoons honey
- 1 teaspoon vanilla extract

Direction

- In a blender, add 1/2 of each ingredients. Cover then process till blended. Do the same with the remaining ingredients. Transfer into chilled glasses and serve at once.

Nutrition Information

- Calories: 143 calories
- Protein: 6g protein. Diabetic Exchanges: 2 fruit
- Total Fat: 0 fat (0 saturated fat)
- Sodium: 69mg sodium
- Fiber: 2g fiber)
- Total Carbohydrate: 34g carbohydrate (28g sugars
- Cholesterol: 3mg cholesterol

41. Blueberry Banana Smoothies

Serving: 3 servings. | Prep: 5mins | Cook: 0mins | Ready in:

Ingredients

- 1 medium ripe banana, cut into chunks
- 1 cup frozen unsweetened blueberries
- 1 cup cherry juice blend
- 3/4 cup vanilla yogurt
- 1/2 cup crushed ice
- Dash ground cinnamon

Direction

- Mix all ingredients in a blender, then cover and blend until smooth, or for half a minute. Transfer into cold glasses and serve promptly.

Nutrition Information

- Calories: 164 calories
- Cholesterol: 6mg cholesterol
- Protein: 4g protein.
- Total Fat: 2g fat (1g saturated fat)
- Sodium: 44mg sodium
- Fiber: 2g fiber)
- Total Carbohydrate: 33g carbohydrate (26g sugars

42. Blueberry Fruit Smoothie

Serving: 3 servings. | Prep: 5mins | Cook: 0mins | Ready in:

Ingredients

- 1 cup reduced-fat vanilla ice cream
- 1 cup fresh or frozen blueberries
- 1/2 cup chopped peeled fresh peaches or frozen unsweetened sliced peaches
- 1/2 cup pineapple juice

- 1/4 cup vanilla yogurt

Direction

- Mix all ingredients in a blender, then cover and blend until smooth. Transfer into cold glasses and serve promptly.

Nutrition Information

- Calories: 149 calories
- Sodium: 57mg sodium
- Fiber: 2g fiber
- Total Carbohydrate: 30g carbohydrate (0 sugars
- Cholesterol: 7mg cholesterol
- Protein: 3g protein. Diabetic Exchanges: 2 fruit
- Total Fat: 2g fat (1g saturated fat)

43. Blueberry Mango Smoothies

Serving: 2 servings. | Prep: 10mins | Cook: 0mins | Ready in:

Ingredients

- 1 cup vanilla soy milk
- 1 small banana, frozen and cut into chunks
- 1/2 cup chopped peeled mango
- 1/4 cup fresh or frozen unsweetened blueberries
- 3 ounces silken firm tofu
- 1 tablespoon sugar
- 1/2 teaspoon vanilla extract

Direction

- Mix all ingredients in a blender, then cover and blend until combined. Transfer into cold glasses and serve promptly.

Nutrition Information

- Calories: 185 calories
- Total Carbohydrate: 34g carbohydrate (24g sugars
- Cholesterol: 0 cholesterol
- Protein: 7g protein.
- Total Fat: 3g fat (0 saturated fat)
- Sodium: 64mg sodium
- Fiber: 3g fiber)

44. Blueberry Milk Shake

Serving: 3-4 servings. | Prep: 10mins | Cook: 0mins | Ready in:

Ingredients

- 1 cup whole milk
- 2 tablespoons lemon juice
- 1 pint vanilla ice cream
- 1 cup fresh or frozen blueberries
- 1 tablespoon sugar
- 1 tablespoon grated lemon zest

Direction

- Combine all the ingredients in the container of the blender. Cover it and process on High speed until smooth. Pour the mixture into the glasses. You can refrigerate any leftovers.

Nutrition Information

- Calories: 205 calories
- Cholesterol: 37mg cholesterol
- Protein: 5g protein.
- Total Fat: 9g fat (6g saturated fat)
- Sodium: 83mg sodium
- Fiber: 1g fiber)
- Total Carbohydrate: 28g carbohydrate (21g sugars

45. Blueberry Orange Blast

Serving: 4 servings. | Prep: 5mins | Cook: 0mins | Ready in:

Ingredients

- 1 cup orange juice
- 1 cup (8 ounces) vanilla yogurt
- 1 medium banana, sliced and frozen
- 1 cup frozen unsweetened blueberries
- 1/2 cup silken firm tofu

Direction

- Mix all ingredients in a blender, then cover and blend until smooth. Transfer into cold glasses and serve promptly.

Nutrition Information

- Calories: 140 calories
- Cholesterol: 3mg cholesterol
- Protein: 5g protein. Diabetic Exchanges: 1 starch
- Total Fat: 2g fat (1g saturated fat)
- Sodium: 49mg sodium
- Fiber: 2g fiber)
- Total Carbohydrate: 27g carbohydrate (22g sugars

46. Blueberry Orange Smoothies

Serving: 4 servings. | Prep: 10mins | Cook: 0mins | Ready in:

Ingredients

- 2 medium navel oranges
- 1 cup fat-free plain yogurt
- 1/4 cup fat-free milk
- 2/3 cup fresh or frozen blueberries
- 4 teaspoons sugar
- 1 to 1-1/3 cups ice cubes

Direction

- Peel oranges and get rid of all white pith, then divide into sections. Put in a blender, then add in sugar, blueberries, milk and yogurt. Cover and blend until smooth. Put in ice, then cover and blend again until smooth. Transfer into cold glasses and serve promptly.

Nutrition Information

- Calories: 92 calories
- Sodium: 43mg sodium
- Fiber: 2g fiber)
- Total Carbohydrate: 21g carbohydrate (17g sugars
- Cholesterol: 2mg cholesterol
- Protein: 4g protein. Diabetic Exchanges: 1-1/2 fruit.
- Total Fat: 0 fat (0 saturated fat)

47. Blueberry Oat Smoothies

Serving: 3 servings. | Prep: 10mins | Cook: 0mins | Ready in:

Ingredients

- 1 cup unsweetened apple juice
- 1 cup vanilla yogurt
- 1 cup frozen unsweetened blueberries
- 1/2 cup quick-cooking oats
- 2 tablespoons maple syrup

Direction

- Mix all ingredients in a blender then cover and blend until smooth, about a half minute. Transfer into cold glasses and serve promptly.

Nutrition Information

- Calories: 219 calories
- Sodium: 58mg sodium

- Fiber: 3g fiber)
- Total Carbohydrate: 45g carbohydrate (33g sugars
- Cholesterol: 4mg cholesterol
- Protein: 6g protein.
- Total Fat: 2g fat (1g saturated fat)

48. Bourbon Slush

Serving: 14 | Prep: 10mins | Cook: | Ready in:

Ingredients

- 1 (6 ounce) can frozen orange juice concentrate
- 1 (12 ounce) can frozen lemonade concentrate
- 1 (46 fluid ounce) can pineapple juice
- 1 1/2 cups white sugar
- 2 cups strong brewed black tea
- 2 cups bourbon whiskey
- 1 (2 liter) bottle lemon-lime flavored carbonated beverage

Direction

- Combine together whisky, tea, sugar, pineapple juice, lemonade concentrate and orange juice concentrate in a big bowl or container. Turn the mixture to a shallow dishes or bowls and put in the freezer to chill overnight.
- Take the frozen mixture out of the freezer and allow it to stand for 10 minutes. Use a potato masher or a wire whisk to chop until slushy consistency forms. Scoop out the frozen slush into glasses and pour lemon-lime flavored soda on top.

49. Brandy Slush

Serving: 21 servings (about 4 quarts slush mix). | Prep: 10mins | Cook: 5mins | Ready in:

Ingredients

- 4 individual green or black tea bags
- 9 cups water, divided
- 2 cups brandy
- 1 can (12 ounces) frozen lemonade concentrate, thawed
- 1 can (12 ounces) frozen orange juice concentrate, thawed
- EACH SERVING:
- 1/4 cup lemon-lime soda, chilled
- GARNISH:
- Lime wedge, optional

Direction

- In a small bowl, place tea bags. Boil 2 cups of water then pour over the tea bags. Cover and let steep for 5 minutes. Remove the tea bags. Pour into a larger pitcher then stir in the leftover water, juice concentrate, lemonade concentrate and brandy. Transfer into a 4-quart freezer container then store in the freeze overnight to set.
- To prepare each serving, scoop and place 3/4 cup of slush into a rocks glass. Add in lemon-lime soda and (if preferred) add lime wedge to serve.

Nutrition Information

- Calories: 129 calories
- Protein: 0 protein.
- Total Fat: 0 fat (0 saturated fat)
- Sodium: 8mg sodium
- Fiber: 0 fiber)
- Total Carbohydrate: 20g carbohydrate (19g sugars
- Cholesterol: 0 cholesterol

50. Breakfast Wassail

Serving: about 4 quarts. | Prep: 5mins | Cook: 60mins | Ready in:

Ingredients

- 1 can (64 ounces) cranberry juice
- 1 can (32 ounces) apple juice
- 1 can (12 ounces) frozen pineapple juice concentrate, undiluted
- 1 can (12 ounces) frozen lemonade concentrate, undiluted
- 3 to 4 cinnamon sticks
- 1 quart water, optional

Direction

- Mix cinnamon sticks, lemonade, and juices together in a Dutch oven or a big pot; boil. Lower heat and let it simmer, covered, for an hour. If preferred, add water. Serve wassail cold or hot.

Nutrition Information

- Calories: 156 calories
- Cholesterol: 0 cholesterol
- Protein: 1g protein.
- Total Fat: 0 fat (0 saturated fat)
- Sodium: 5mg sodium
- Fiber: 0 fiber)
- Total Carbohydrate: 40g carbohydrate (38g sugars

51. Buttermilk Boost

Serving: 2 servings. | Prep: 5mins | Cook: 0mins | Ready in:

Ingredients

- 1 cup buttermilk
- 1/4 cup chilled orange juice
- 1/4 cup chilled unsweetened pineapple juice
- 2 tablespoons sugar
- 1 teaspoon lemon juice

Direction

- Blend all the ingredients in a blender until well-combined. Pour it into the chilled glasses and serve them immediately.

Nutrition Information

- Calories: 129 calories
- Total Carbohydrate: 26g carbohydrate (25g sugars
- Cholesterol: 5mg cholesterol
- Protein: 4g protein. Diabetic Exchanges: 1 starch
- Total Fat: 1g fat (1g saturated fat)
- Sodium: 129mg sodium
- Fiber: 0 fiber)

52. Buttermilk Ice Cream Shake

Serving: 3 servings. | Prep: 10mins | Cook: 0mins | Ready in:

Ingredients

- 3 cups chilled buttermilk
- 1/2 cup cold lemon juice
- Pinch of salt
- 1/2 cup sugar
- 1/8 teaspoon grated lemon zest
- 1 cup vanilla ice cream
- Dash ginger

Direction

- Blend or shake all of the ingredients. Serve the shake together with the ginger.

Nutrition Information

- Calories: 326 calories
- Total Fat: 7g fat (4g saturated fat)
- Sodium: 342mg sodium
- Fiber: 0 fiber)
- Total Carbohydrate: 59g carbohydrate (53g sugars

- Cholesterol: 29mg cholesterol
- Protein: 10g protein.

53. Buttermilk Shake

Serving: 2 servings. | Prep: 5mins | Cook: 0mins | Ready in:

Ingredients

- 1 pint vanilla ice cream
- 1 cup buttermilk
- 1 teaspoon grated lemon zest
- 1/2 teaspoon vanilla extract
- 1 drop lemon extract

Direction

- In a blender container, combine all the ingredients and process them on high speed until smooth. Pour the drink into the glasses. Make sure to put all the leftovers inside the refrigerator.

Nutrition Information

- Calories: 317 calories
- Fiber: 0 fiber)
- Total Carbohydrate: 37g carbohydrate (29g sugars
- Cholesterol: 63mg cholesterol
- Protein: 9g protein.
- Total Fat: 16g fat (10g saturated fat)
- Sodium: 234mg sodium

54. Candy Apple Martini

Serving: 1 | Prep: 5mins | Cook: | Ready in:

Ingredients

- 1 fluid ounce vanilla vodka
- 1 fluid ounce sour apple schnapps
- 1 fluid ounce butterscotch schnapps
- 1 fluid ounce cranberry juice
- 1 maraschino cherry

Direction

- Pour cranberry juice, butterscotch schnapps, apple schnapps and vodka over ice in a cocktail shaker. Cover and shake till it's frosty on the outside of the shaker. Into a chilled martini glass, strain the drink. Use a maraschino cherry to garnish and serve.

55. Cantaloupe Banana Smoothies

Serving: 3 servings. | Prep: 10mins | Cook: 0mins | Ready in:

Ingredients

- 1/2 cup fat-free plain yogurt
- 4-1/2 teaspoons orange juice concentrate
- 2 cups cubed cantaloupe
- 1 large firm banana, cut into 1-inch pieces and frozen
- 2 tablespoons nonfat dry milk powder
- 2 teaspoons honey

Direction

- Mix all ingredients in a blender. Cover and blend until combined, then transfer into cold glasses and serve promptly.

Nutrition Information

- Calories: 141 calories
- Sodium: 60mg sodium
- Fiber: 2g fiber)
- Total Carbohydrate: 32g carbohydrate (26g sugars
- Cholesterol: 2mg cholesterol
- Protein: 5g protein. Diabetic Exchanges: 1 starch

- Total Fat: 1g fat (0 saturated fat)

56. Cantaloupe Orange Milk Shakes

Serving: 2 servings. | Prep: 10mins | Cook: 0mins | Ready in:

Ingredients

- 4-1/2 teaspoons orange juice concentrate
- 3/4 cup cubed cantaloupe
- 1 cup vanilla ice cream or frozen yogurt
- 3/4 cup milk
- 3 tablespoons sugar

Direction

- Mix cantaloupe and orange juice concentrate in a blender. Cover the blender and process it until smooth. Add the sugar, milk, and ice cream. Cover again and process until well-blended. Pour the mixture into the chilled glasses and serve.

Nutrition Information

- Calories: 304 calories
- Cholesterol: 41mg cholesterol
- Protein: 6g protein.
- Total Fat: 11g fat (6g saturated fat)
- Sodium: 104mg sodium
- Fiber: 1g fiber)
- Total Carbohydrate: 49g carbohydrate (44g sugars

57. Cappuccino Shake

Serving: 1 serving. | Prep: 10mins | Cook: 0mins | Ready in:

Ingredients

- 1 cup fat-free milk
- 1-1/2 teaspoons instant coffee granules
- Sugar substitute equivalent to 4 teaspoons sugar
- 2 drops brandy extract or rum extract
- Dash ground cinnamon

Direction

- Combine the extract, coffee granules, milk, and sweetener in a blender. Blend the mixture until the coffee is dissolved. Serve it together with a dash of cinnamon. In case you wanted to serve it hot, pour the drink into the mug and let it warm in a microwave.

Nutrition Information

- Calories: 100 calories
- Sodium: 128mg sodium
- Fiber: 0 fiber)
- Total Carbohydrate: 15g carbohydrate (0 sugars
- Cholesterol: 4mg cholesterol
- Protein: 9g protein. Diabetic Exchanges: 1 fat-free milk.
- Total Fat: 0 fat (0 saturated fat)

58. Champagne Blood Shots

Serving: 18 servings. | Prep: 30mins | Cook: 0mins | Ready in:

Ingredients

- 3/4 cup sugar, divided
- 1/4 cup water
- 1/4 cup sliced fresh gingerroot
- 2 envelopes unflavored gelatin
- 1-1/2 cups cold water
- 1-1/2 cups chilled Champagne
- 2 cups fresh strawberries, hulled and quartered
- Red food coloring, optional

Direction

- Combine ginger, water and 1/4 cup of sugar in a small saucepan then boil. Lower the heat and let simmer for 3-5 minutes, uncovered, stir occasionally till sugar dissolves. Take away from the heat and let cool to room temperature. Drain and remove ginger.
- Sprinkle over cold water with gelatin in a small saucepan and allow to stand for 1 minute. Over low heat, heat and stir to completely dissolve the gelatin. Stir in the leftover sugar. Cook and stir to dissolve the sugar. Take away from the heat then add in champagne and stir. Transfer into 18 2-oz. tall shot glasses. Store in the fridge for 25 minutes to set partially.
- In the meantime, blend strawberries in a food process till blended. Place into a small bowl then add in 2 tbsp. of cooled simple syrup and stir. The leftover syrup can be removed and reserved for other uses. Tint red if preferred.
- For blood in gelatin, add strawberry mixture to fill a clean eye dropper. Place into the gelatin that has partially set and release the strawberry mixture by squeezing while pulling the dropper upward. Store in the fridge till firm.

Nutrition Information

- Calories: 54 calories
- Sodium: 2mg sodium
- Fiber: 0 fiber)
- Total Carbohydrate: 10g carbohydrate (9g sugars
- Cholesterol: 0 cholesterol
- Protein: 1g protein.
- Total Fat: 0 fat (0 saturated fat)

59. Champagne Party Punch

Serving: 18 servings (3/4 cup each). | Prep: 15mins | Cook: 0mins | Ready in:

Ingredients

- 1 cup sugar
- 1 cup water
- 2 cups unsweetened apple juice
- 2 cups unsweetened pineapple juice
- 1/2 cup lemon juice
- 1/3 cup thawed orange juice concentrate
- 1/4 cup lime juice
- 2 cups ice cubes
- 1 quart ginger ale, chilled
- 1 bottle (750 ml) champagne, chilled

Direction

- Combine water and sugar in a large pitcher till sugar dissolves. Pour in lime juice, orange juice concentrate, lemon juice, pineapple juice and apple juice. Store in the fridge till serving.
- Transfer into a punch bowl and place in ice cubes right before serving. Add in champagne and ginger ale gradually.

Nutrition Information

- Calories: 129 calories
- Cholesterol: 0 cholesterol
- Protein: 0 protein.
- Total Fat: 0 fat (0 saturated fat)
- Sodium: 8mg sodium
- Fiber: 0 fiber)
- Total Carbohydrate: 26g carbohydrate (25g sugars

60. Cheery Cranberry Nog

Serving: 3 quarts. | Prep: 10mins | Cook: 15mins | Ready in:

Ingredients

- 2 cups half-and-half cream
- 6 eggs
- 1 cup sugar
- 3 cups heavy whipping cream

- 2 cans (11-1/2 ounces each) thawed cranberry juice concentrate, undiluted
- 2 cups water

Direction

- Mix eggs, sugar and half-and-half together in a Dutch oven. Cook the mixture over medium heat and stir until it is 160°F in temperature or until it achieves a thick consistency that coats the back of a spoon. Remove the mixture from heat and allow it to cool down a bit. Add in the remaining ingredients. Cover the mixture and place it in the fridge until cold.

Nutrition Information

- Calories: 415 calories
- Total Fat: 29g fat (17g saturated fat)
- Sodium: 75mg sodium
- Fiber: 0 fiber)
- Total Carbohydrate: 34g carbohydrate (31g sugars
- Cholesterol: 208mg cholesterol
- Protein: 6g protein.

61. Cherry Chip Shakes

Serving: 2 servings. | Prep: 5mins | Cook: 0mins | Ready in:

Ingredients

- 3 cups vanilla ice cream or frozen vanilla yogurt
- 3 tablespoons hot fudge ice cream topping
- 1/4 cup miniature chocolate chips
- 4 maraschino cherries
- Whipped topping and additional cherries

Direction

- Combine the cherries, fudge topping, ice cream, and chocolate chips in a blender. Cover and blend the mixture until well-combined.

Pour it into the tall glasses and top it with a dollop of whipped topping and a cherry.

Nutrition Information

- Calories: 619 calories
- Fiber: 2g fiber)
- Total Carbohydrate: 84g carbohydrate (64g sugars
- Cholesterol: 87mg cholesterol
- Protein: 9g protein.
- Total Fat: 30g fat (18g saturated fat)
- Sodium: 198mg sodium

62. Cherry Chocolate Floats

Serving: 7 servings. | Prep: 25mins | Cook: 5mins | Ready in:

Ingredients

- 1 cup water
- 3/4 cup sugar
- 2 cups carbonated water, chilled
- 3 tablespoons maraschino cherry juice
- Chocolate syrup
- 14 scoops chocolate ice cream
- Whipped cream in a can
- 7 maraschino cherries

Direction

- Boil sugar and water in a large saucepan. Lower the heat and let it simmer for 5 minutes. Allow it to cool. Mix in cherry juice and carbonated water.
- Place chocolate syrup in each of the seven chilled glasses. Fill each glass with two scoops of ice cream. Drizzle carbonated water mixture over the ice cream. Top each drink with a cherry and whipped cream. Serve them right away.

Nutrition Information

- Calories: 240 calories
- Total Fat: 7g fat (4g saturated fat)
- Sodium: 51mg sodium
- Fiber: 1g fiber)
- Total Carbohydrate: 44g carbohydrate (43g sugars
- Cholesterol: 22mg cholesterol
- Protein: 3g protein.

63. Cherry Cobbler Smoothies

Serving: 5 servings. | Prep: 10mins | Cook: 0mins | Ready in:

Ingredients

- 2 cups vanilla yogurt
- 1/2 cup orange juice
- 1/4 cup honey
- 1 teaspoon vanilla extract
- 1 teaspoon almond extract
- 2 cups ice cubes
- 2 cups frozen pitted dark sweet cherries
- 2 teaspoons ground cinnamon

Direction

- Mix all ingredients in a blender, then cover and blend until smooth, about a half minute. Transfer into cold glasses. Serve promptly.

Nutrition Information

- Calories: 197 calories
- Protein: 6g protein.
- Total Fat: 2g fat (1g saturated fat)
- Sodium: 66mg sodium
- Fiber: 2g fiber)
- Total Carbohydrate: 40g carbohydrate (38g sugars
- Cholesterol: 5mg cholesterol

64. Cherry Yogurt Smoothies

Serving: 4 servings. | Prep: 5mins | Cook: 0mins | Ready in:

Ingredients

- 1 cup cranberry juice
- 1 cup (8 ounces) cherry yogurt
- 1/2 cup cherry pie filling
- 1 medium ripe banana, cut into chunks
- 1 to 1-1/2 cups ice cubes

Direction

- Mix all ingredients in a blender, then cover and blend until combined. Transfer into cold glasses and serve promptly.

Nutrition Information

- Calories: 150 calories
- Sodium: 38mg sodium
- Fiber: 1g fiber)
- Total Carbohydrate: 34g carbohydrate (32g sugars
- Cholesterol: 3mg cholesterol
- Protein: 3g protein.
- Total Fat: 1g fat (0 saturated fat)

65. Cherry Berry Soy Smoothies

Serving: 3 servings. | Prep: 10mins | Cook: 0mins | Ready in:

Ingredients

- 1 cup vanilla soy milk
- 1/2 cup vanilla soy yogurt
- 2 teaspoons honey
- 1 cup fresh or frozen pitted dark sweet cherries
- 1/2 cup fresh or frozen blueberries
- 1/2 cup crushed ice

Direction

- Combine all of the ingredients in a blender. Cover and blend till smooth, for 30-45 seconds.
- Stir as needed. Transfer into chilled glasses. Serve at once.

Nutrition Information

- Calories: 130 calories
- Protein: 4g protein. Diabetic Exchanges: 1 fruit
- Total Fat: 2g fat (0 saturated fat)
- Sodium: 41mg sodium
- Fiber: 3g fiber)
- Total Carbohydrate: 24g carbohydrate (20g sugars
- Cholesterol: 0 cholesterol

66. Chilled Lemon Coffees

Serving: 3 servings. | Prep: 10mins | Cook: 0mins | Ready in:

Ingredients

- 2 cups strong brewed coffee (French or other dark roast), chilled
- 1 cup lemon sherbet, softened
- 2 tablespoons sugar
- 1 tablespoon lemon juice
- Lemon peel, optional

Direction

- In a blender, add lemon juice, sugar, sherbet and coffee. Cover and process till smooth. Transfer into chilled glasses. Add lemon peel to garnish if preferred. Immediately serve.

Nutrition Information

- Calories: 105 calories
- Cholesterol: 3mg cholesterol
- Protein: 1g protein.
- Total Fat: 1g fat (1g saturated fat)
- Sodium: 26mg sodium
- Fiber: 0 fiber)
- Total Carbohydrate: 24g carbohydrate (20g sugars

67. Chilled Mocha Eggnog

Serving: 4 servings. | Prep: 10mins | Cook: 0mins | Ready in:

Ingredients

- 1-1/2 teaspoons instant coffee granules
- 1 tablespoon hot water
- 4 cups eggnog
- 2 tablespoons brown sugar
- 1/8 teaspoon ground cinnamon
- 1/2 cup heavy whipping cream
- 2 tablespoons confectioners' sugar
- 1/2 teaspoon vanilla extract
- Additional ground cinnamon, optional

Direction

- Dissolve coffee in water in a pitcher. Whisk in cinnamon, the eggnog and brown sugar; until sugar is dissolved. Let it chill.
- Whisk the cream, vanilla and confectioners' sugar in a small bowl until soft peaks form. Put eggnog mixture into glasses; add whipped cream on the top. Dust cinnamon on the top if desired.

Nutrition Information

- Calories: 488 calories
- Protein: 10g protein.
- Total Fat: 30g fat (18g saturated fat)
- Sodium: 151mg sodium
- Fiber: 0 fiber)
- Total Carbohydrate: 46g carbohydrate (45g sugars
- Cholesterol: 191mg cholesterol

68. Chocolate Banana Smoothies

Serving: 4 servings. | Prep: 5mins | Cook: 0mins | Ready in:

Ingredients

- 2 cups cold 2% milk
- 1 package (1.4 ounces) sugar-free instant chocolate pudding mix
- 2 tablespoons vanilla extract
- 2 large ripe frozen bananas, sliced
- 2 cups coarsely crushed ice cubes

Direction

- Combine vanilla, pudding mix and milk in a blender; cover then blend till blended. Place in ice and bananas; cover and blend till smooth. Transfer into chilled glasses and serve at once.

Nutrition Information

- Calories: 166 calories
- Cholesterol: 10mg cholesterol
- Protein: 6g protein. Diabetic Exchanges: 1 fruit
- Total Fat: 3g fat (2g saturated fat)
- Sodium: 360mg sodium
- Fiber: 2g fiber)
- Total Carbohydrate: 31g carbohydrate (0 sugars

69. Chocolate Coffee

Serving: 12 servings. | Prep: 20mins | Cook: 40mins | Ready in:

Ingredients

- 1 cup sugar
- 1 cup baking cocoa
- 1 cup boiling water
- 1 teaspoon vanilla extract
- 1/4 teaspoon salt
- 4 cups heavy whipping cream, whipped
- 8 cups hot strong brewed coffee or whole milk

Direction

- Whisk water, cocoa and sugar together in a big heavy saucepan till smooth. Over medium-low heat, cook and whisk for 35 minutes till soft peaks form when you lift up the whisk and the mixture looks like hot fudge sauce. Take away from the heat. Mix in salt and vanilla. Pour into a bowl and leave in the fridge for at least 2 hours.
- Beat the chocolate mixture. Mix in well 2 cups of whipped cream. Fold in the leftover whipped cream. Add about 1/2 cup of chocolate cream into 2/3 cup of milk or coffee for each serving. Stir till blended.

Nutrition Information

- Calories: 362 calories
- Cholesterol: 109mg cholesterol
- Protein: 3g protein.
- Total Fat: 30g fat (18g saturated fat)
- Sodium: 83mg sodium
- Fiber: 1g fiber)
- Total Carbohydrate: 24g carbohydrate (18g sugars

70. Chocolate Malts

Serving: 2-1/2 cups. | Prep: 10mins | Cook: 0mins | Ready in:

Ingredients

- 3/4 cup milk
- 1/2 cup caramel ice cream topping
- 2 cups chocolate ice cream, softened
- 3 tablespoons malted milk powder

- 2 tablespoons chopped pecans, optional
- Grated chocolate, optional

Direction

- Combine the first five ingredients in a blender. Cover and process the mixture until blended. Pour the mixture into the chilled glasses. If desired, sprinkle it with grated chocolate. Serve them immediately.

Nutrition Information

- Calories: 628 calories
- Sodium: 517mg sodium
- Fiber: 2g fiber)
- Total Carbohydrate: 113g carbohydrate (101g sugars
- Cholesterol: 62mg cholesterol
- Protein: 11g protein.
- Total Fat: 18g fat (11g saturated fat)

71. Chocolaty Banana Smoothie

Serving: 2 servings. | Prep: 10mins | Cook: 0mins | Ready in:

Ingredients

- 1 cup chocolate milk
- 1/2 cup plain yogurt
- 1 medium banana, peeled, cut into chunks and frozen
- 1 teaspoon honey
- 1/2 teaspoon vanilla extract
- 1 cup ice cubes

Direction

- Mix together vanilla, honey, banana, yogurt and milk in a blender, then cover and blend until smooth. Put in ice cubes then cover and blend until combined. Transfer into cold glasses and serve promptly.

Nutrition Information

- Calories: 208 calories
- Total Carbohydrate: 33g carbohydrate (28g sugars
- Cholesterol: 23mg cholesterol
- Protein: 7g protein.
- Total Fat: 7g fat (4g saturated fat)
- Sodium: 104mg sodium
- Fiber: 2g fiber)

72. Christmas Glow Punch

Serving: About 2 quarts. | Prep: 10mins | Cook: 0mins | Ready in:

Ingredients

- 4-1/2 cups tropical punch
- 1 cup cranberry juice
- 1 can (6 ounces) pineapple juice
- 1/3 cup lemon juice
- 2 to 3 cups chilled ginger ale
- 1 pint raspberry sherbet

Direction

- Combine juices and punch in a 2-quart container. Store in the fridge to chill, covered. Place into a small punch bowl right before serving. Add in ginger ale and stir; place scoops of sherbet on top.

Nutrition Information

- Calories: 103 calories
- Protein: 0 protein. Diabetic Exchanges: 1-1/2 starch.
- Total Fat: 0 fat (0 saturated fat)
- Sodium: 22mg sodium
- Fiber: 0 fiber)
- Total Carbohydrate: 25g carbohydrate (23g sugars
- Cholesterol: 1mg cholesterol

73. Cinnamon Apple Shakes

Serving: 4 servings. | Prep: 10mins | Cook: 0mins | Ready in:

Ingredients

- 3 cups vanilla ice cream
- 3/4 cup 2% milk
- 1/2 cup cinnamon applesauce
- 1/4 cup caramel ice cream topping
- 1/2 teaspoon rum extract

Direction

- Combine all the ingredients in a blender. Cover and process it until the mixture is smooth. Pour it into the chilled glasses and serve.

Nutrition Information

- Calories: 300 calories
- Total Fat: 12g fat (7g saturated fat)
- Sodium: 175mg sodium
- Fiber: 1g fiber)
- Total Carbohydrate: 45g carbohydrate (25g sugars
- Cholesterol: 47mg cholesterol
- Protein: 5g protein.

74. Citrus Cooler

Serving: Serves 4 | Prep: | Cook: | Ready in:

Ingredients

- 1 cup water
- 1/4 cup sugar
- 1 cup fresh orange juice
- 1 cup fresh grapefruit juice
- 1/4 cup fresh lime juice
- 2 tablespoons fresh lemon juice
- Ice cubes

Direction

- In a small saucepan, stir in sugar and 1 cup water on medium low heat until sugar is dissolved. Bring the mixture to a boil. Turn the syrup to a pitcher and place in fridge to refrigerate until chilled. Put in the pitcher with lemon juice, lime juice, grapefruit juice and orange juice and stir to mix. (You can prepare 1 day in advance and keep chilled.) Fill ice into 4 glasses then pour over ice with citrus cooler and serve.

75. Citrus Frost

Serving: 2 servings. | Prep: 10mins | Cook: 0mins | Ready in:

Ingredients

- 1 can (8 ounces) crushed pineapple, undrained
- 1 cup orange juice
- 1/3 cup sugar
- 2 tablespoons lime juice
- 2 tablespoons lemon juice
- 1-1/4 cups vanilla ice cream

Direction

- Combine the first five ingredients in a blender. Cover the blender and blend the mixture on high speed until smooth. Add the ice cream and blend it again until combined. Pour the drink into the chilled glasses and serve.

Nutrition Information

- Calories: 426 calories
- Fiber: 1g fiber)
- Total Carbohydrate: 86g carbohydrate (73g sugars
- Cholesterol: 36mg cholesterol
- Protein: 4g protein.

- Total Fat: 9g fat (6g saturated fat)
- Sodium: 68mg sodium

76. Citrus Iced Tea

Serving: 4 | Prep: | Cook: 10mins | Ready in:

Ingredients

- ½ cup lemon juice
- ⅓ cup sugar, or to taste
- 3½ cups strong brewed tea

Direction

- In a pitcher, stir sugar and lemon juice together to dissolve the sugar. Add in tea and stir. Let chill.

Nutrition Information

- Calories: 72 calories;
- Total Carbohydrate: 19
- Total Fat: 0
- Saturated Fat: 0
- Fiber: 0
- Sugar: 18
- Protein: 0
- Sodium: 0
- Cholesterol: 0

77. Citrus Iced Tea With Mint

Serving: 8 servings. | Prep: 20mins | Cook: 0mins | Ready in:

Ingredients

- 8 cups water, divided
- 6 individual tea bags
- 1 to 2 mint sprigs
- 3-1/2 teaspoons Crystal Light lemonade drink mix
- 2 cups orange juice
- Ice cubes

Direction

- Boil 1 quart of water in a Dutch oven. Place in mint and tea bags. Cover then let steep for 10 minutes. Strain to remove mint and tea bags.
- Combine the leftover water and lemonade mix in a large container. Add in orange juice and tea then stir. Let cool and pour over ice to serve.

Nutrition Information

- Calories: 32 calories
- Total Fat: 0 fat (0 saturated fat)
- Sodium: 1mg sodium
- Fiber: 0 fiber)
- Total Carbohydrate: 7g carbohydrate (6g sugars
- Cholesterol: 0 cholesterol
- Protein: 0 protein. Diabetic Exchanges: 1/2 fruit.

78. Citrus Mint Cooler

Serving: about 15 servings. | Prep: 30mins | Cook: 0mins | Ready in:

Ingredients

- 2-1/2 cups water
- 2 cups sugar
- 1 cup lemon juice (about 6 lemons)
- 1 cup orange juice (about 6 oranges)
- 10 mint sprigs
- 1 bottle (32 ounces) ginger ale, chilled
- Cold water
- Ice cubes

Direction

- In a big saucepan, put the first 5 ingredients; boil it, whisking until the sugar dissolves. Put a cover on; take away from the heat and steep until cool. Drain. Put a cover on and chill.
- For serving, fill equal amounts of water, ginger ale and fruit juice into a pitcher or cold glasses. Add ice and enjoy immediately.

Nutrition Information

- Calories: 137 calories
- Protein: 0 protein.
- Total Fat: 0 fat (0 saturated fat)
- Sodium: 5mg sodium
- Fiber: 0 fiber)
- Total Carbohydrate: 35g carbohydrate (33g sugars
- Cholesterol: 0 cholesterol

79. Citrus Punch

Serving: 12 servings, 1 cup each | Prep: 10mins | Cook: | Ready in:

Ingredients

- 1 can (12 oz.) frozen orange juice concentrate (Do not thaw.)
- 1-1/4 qt. (5 cups) cold water
- 1 pkt. (makes 2 qt. drink) or 2 pkt. (makes 1 qt. drink each) CRYSTAL LIGHT Lemonade Flavor Drink Mix*
- 1 bottle (1 L) club soda
- 1 navel orange, thinly sliced

Direction

- In a 2-quart glass or plastic pitcher with drink mix, pour water and juice concentrate; mix until the mix fully dissolves. Chill for 30 minutes.
- Add to punch bowl right before enjoying. Mix in club soda. Add orange slices.
- Enjoy over ice.

Nutrition Information

- Calories: 50
- Total Fat: 0 g
- Cholesterol: 0 mg
- Protein: 1 g
- Sodium: 45 mg
- Fiber: 0 g
- Sugar: 11 g
- Total Carbohydrate: 12 g
- Saturated Fat: 0 g

80. Citrus Quencher

Serving: 3 quarts. | Prep: 10mins | Cook: 0mins | Ready in:

Ingredients

- 1 cup lemon juice
- 1 cup lime juice
- 1 cup sugar
- 1 container (64 ounces) orange juice
- 2 cups club soda, chilled
- Lime slices, optional

Direction

- Combine sugar, lime juice and lemon juice in a large container or pitcher; stir to dissolve. Add in orange juice and stir. Store in the fridge till serving. Place in ice cubes and soda. Add lime for garnish if preferred.

Nutrition Information

- Calories: 148 calories
- Sodium: 9mg sodium
- Fiber: 0 fiber)
- Total Carbohydrate: 38g carbohydrate (32g sugars
- Cholesterol: 0 cholesterol
- Protein: 1g protein.
- Total Fat: 0 fat (0 saturated fat)

81. Citrus Tea Punch

Serving: 3 quarts. | Prep: 20mins | Cook: 0mins | Ready in:

Ingredients

- 6 individual tea bags
- 6 cups boiling water
- 1-1/2 cups sugar
- 3 cups chilled club soda
- 2 cups orange juice
- 1 cup lemon juice
- Crushed ice
- Orange and lemon slices
- Fresh mint sprigs, optional

Direction

- Let tea bags steep for 15 minutes in boiling water. Remove bags. Add in sugar and stir to dissolve. Add lemon juice, orange juice and soda then mix well. Store in the fridge to chill.
- Pour over ice to serve. Add mint, lemon slices and orange for garnish if desired.

Nutrition Information

- Calories: 120 calories
- Total Carbohydrate: 31g carbohydrate (29g sugars)
- Cholesterol: 0 cholesterol
- Protein: 0 protein.
- Total Fat: 0 fat (0 saturated fat)
- Sodium: 13mg sodium
- Fiber: 0 fiber)

82. Coffee Milk

Serving: Makes 1 serving. | Prep: 5mins | Cook: | Ready in:

Ingredients

- 1 tsp. MAXWELL HOUSE Instant Coffee
- 1 cup milk
- ice cubes

Direction

- In a tall glass, place the instant coffee.
- Pour in a small amount of milk then stir to dissolve the coffee.
- Stir in the leftover milk then place in ice cubes. If preferred, sweeten to taste.

Nutrition Information

- Calories: 120
- Cholesterol: 20 mg
- Protein: 8 g
- Total Fat: 5 g
- Saturated Fat: 2.5 g
- Fiber: 0 g
- Sugar: 12 g
- Sodium: 115 mg
- Total Carbohydrate: 12 g

83. Coffee Punch

Serving: 13 servings (2-1/2 quarts). | Prep: 15mins | Cook: 0mins | Ready in:

Ingredients

- 4 cups brewed vanilla-flavored coffee, cooled
- 1 can (12 ounces) evaporated milk
- 1/2 cup sugar
- 1/2 gallon vanilla ice cream, softened
- Ground cinnamon

Direction

- Combine sugar, milk and coffee in a big container till sugar dissolves. Scoop ice cream into a punch bowl. Add coffee mixture over the top. Drizzle with cinnamon and immediately serve.

Nutrition Information

- Calories: 228 calories
- Total Carbohydrate: 30g carbohydrate (24g sugars
- Cholesterol: 44mg cholesterol
- Protein: 5g protein.
- Total Fat: 11g fat (7g saturated fat)
- Sodium: 91mg sodium
- Fiber: 0 fiber)

84. Cola Floats

Serving: 4 servings. | Prep: 5mins | Cook: 0mins | Ready in:

Ingredients

- 4 cups cherry cola, chilled
- 1 teaspoon vanilla extract
- 8 scoops fudge ripple ice cream
- Whipped cream in a can, optional
- 4 maraschino cherries

Direction

- Combine vanilla and cola in a pitcher. In each of 4 chilled glasses, add 2 scoops of ice cream then pour over with cola. Add whipped cream (if desired) and cherries on top.

Nutrition Information

- Calories: 254 calories
- Fiber: 1g fiber)
- Total Carbohydrate: 44g carbohydrate (41g sugars
- Cholesterol: 20mg cholesterol
- Protein: 3g protein.
- Total Fat: 8g fat (5g saturated fat)
- Sodium: 45mg sodium

85. Cool Coffee Refresher

Serving: 2 servings. | Prep: 10mins | Cook: 0mins | Ready in:

Ingredients

- 1 cup strong brewed coffee, chilled
- 1/4 teaspoon vanilla extract
- 1/2 cup vanilla yogurt
- 3 tablespoons sugar
- 1 to 1-1/2 cups ice cubes

Direction

- Combine sugar, yogurt, vanilla and coffee together in a blender. Cover, blend till smooth. Place in ice then cover; process till blended. Transfer into chilled glasses and immediately serve.

Nutrition Information

- Calories: 126 calories
- Sodium: 41mg sodium
- Fiber: 0 fiber)
- Total Carbohydrate: 27g carbohydrate (27g sugars
- Cholesterol: 3mg cholesterol
- Protein: 3g protein. Diabetic Exchanges: 1 starch
- Total Fat: 1g fat (0 saturated fat)

86. Cool Waters Shakes

Serving: 6 servings. | Prep: 10mins | Cook: 0mins | Ready in:

Ingredients

- 4 cups cold milk
- 2 packages (3 ounces each) berry blue gelatin
- 4 cups vanilla ice cream

Direction

- Combine 2 cups of ice cream, one package of gelatin, and 2 cups of milk in a blender. Cover the blender and process the mixture for 30 seconds or until smooth; repeat. Pour the drink into the glasses; serve.

Nutrition Information

- Calories: 328 calories
- Protein: 10g protein.
- Total Fat: 15g fat (9g saturated fat)
- Sodium: 182mg sodium
- Fiber: 0 fiber)
- Total Carbohydrate: 41g carbohydrate (35g sugars
- Cholesterol: 61mg cholesterol

87. Coquito

Serving: 8 | Prep: | Cook: |Ready in:

Ingredients

- 4 cups coconut milk
- 6 tablespoons white sugar
- 8 egg yolks
- 2 teaspoons vanilla extract
- 8 tablespoons dark rum
- 1/2 teaspoon ground nutmeg

Direction

- In a saucepan, mix sugar and coconut milk together and heat the mixture over medium heat until it's scalding.
- Whisk the egg yolks and vanilla together. Put in 1/2 cup of the coconut milk mixture to the egg yolks by beating. Put egg yolk mixture back into coconut milk mixture; then mix. Cook the mixture over low heat while stirring continuously until its temperature hits 160°Fahrenheit (71°Celsius). The mixture should be a thick consistency that coats the back of a spoon. Remember to not bring the mixture to a boil.
- Remove lumps from the eggnog using a strainer and placed over a bowl. Mix in the rum and set aside until it cools down to room temperature. Put plastic wrap over the surface then keep in the fridge until cold. Serve cold with a dash of nutmeg on top.

88. Cran Blueberry Smoothies

Serving: 3 servings. | Prep: 5mins | Cook: 0mins |Ready in:

Ingredients

- 1 cup frozen cranberries
- 1 cup fresh or frozen unsweetened blueberries
- 1 medium banana, cut up
- 1/2 cup 2% milk
- 1/2 cup vanilla yogurt
- 1 tablespoon honey

Direction

- In a blender, add all ingredients, then cover and blend until smooth. Transfer into cold glass and serve promptly.

Nutrition Information

- Calories: 159 calories
- Cholesterol: 5mg cholesterol
- Protein: 4g protein. Diabetic Exchanges: 1 fruit
- Total Fat: 2g fat (1g saturated fat)
- Sodium: 44mg sodium
- Fiber: 4g fiber)
- Total Carbohydrate: 35g carbohydrate (26g sugars

89. Cran Raspberry Iced Tea

Serving: 8 servings. | Prep: 15mins | Cook: 10mins | Ready in:

Ingredients

- 4 cups water
- 1 cup frozen unsweetened raspberries
- 4 teaspoons sugar
- 8 individual raspberry-flavored tea bags
- 4 cups reduced-calorie reduced-sugar cranberry-raspberry juice

Direction

- Boil sugar, raspberries and water in a large saucepan. Lower heat then let simmer for 10 minutes, covered. Take away from the heat then strain and remove the raspberry seeds. Place in tea bags. Allow to stand for 4 minutes. Pour in cranberry-raspberry juice and stir. Pour over ice to serve.

Nutrition Information

- Calories: 38 calories
- Total Carbohydrate: 8g carbohydrate (0 sugars
- Cholesterol: 0 cholesterol
- Protein: 1g protein. Diabetic Exchanges: 1/2 fruit.
- Total Fat: 1g fat (0 saturated fat)
- Sodium: 48mg sodium
- Fiber: 1g fiber)

90. Cranberry Beverage Syrup

Serving: 6 servings. | Prep: 30mins | Cook: 0mins | Ready in:

Ingredients

- 2 quarts water
- 3 pounds fresh or frozen cranberries
- 5 cups sugar
- 5 cinnamon sticks (3 inches)
- ADDITIONAL INGREDIENT FOR CRANBERRY COOLER:
- 1 liter ginger ale, chilled
- ADDITIONAL INGREDIENTS FOR CRAN-APPLE DRINK:
- 2 cups apple juice, chilled
- 2 cups club soda, chilled
- ADDITIONAL INGREDIENTS FOR CRANBERRY-LEMON SPARKLE:
- 1-1/2 quarts cold water
- 1-1/2 quarts ginger ale, chilled
- 1 can (12 ounces) frozen lemonade concentrate, thawed
- ADDITIONAL INGREDIENTS FOR CRANBERRY TEA:
- 2 cups club soda, chilled
- 2 cups iced tea, chilled

Direction

- Boil cinnamon, sugar, cranberries and water in a Dutch oven. Let simmer for 10 minutes, uncovered, till the berries pop. Use a potato masher to slightly mash then simmer for 5 minutes more.
- Strain and remove cinnamon sticks and pulp. Store 2-cup portions of syrup in the fridge for up to 3 days or keep in the freezer for up to 3 months. Thaw then use. Yield 5 batches or about 10 cups in total.
- For Cranberry Cooler: Combine ginger ale and 2 cups of cranberry syrup in a pitcher. Pour over ice to serve. Yield 6 servings.
- For Cranberry-Lemonade Sparkle: Combine lemonade concentrate, 4 cups of cranberry syrup, ginger ale and water in a punch bowl. Pour over ice to serve. Yield 18-20 servings.
- For Cranberry Tea: Combine iced tea, club soda and 2 cups of cranberry syrup in a pitcher, Pour over ice to serve. Yield 6 servings.

Nutrition Information

- Calories: 210 calories
- Sodium: 13mg sodium

- Fiber: 2g fiber)
- Total Carbohydrate: 54g carbohydrate (51g sugars
- Cholesterol: 0 cholesterol
- Protein: 0 protein.
- Total Fat: 0 fat (0 saturated fat)

91. Cranberry Cooler

Serving: 2 servings. | Prep: 5mins | Cook: 0mins | Ready in:

Ingredients

- 1 cup cranberry juice
- 1 cup pineapple juice
- 1/4 cup sugar
- 1/4 teaspoon almond extract
- 1-1/4 cups ginger ale, chilled

Direction

- In a pitcher, mix extract, sugar, and juices. Blend until sugar is dissolved. Let chill in the refrigerator for a minimum of 2 hours. Right before serving, blend in ginger ale.

Nutrition Information

- Calories: 280 calories
- Protein: 1g protein.
- Total Fat: 0 fat (0 saturated fat)
- Sodium: 15mg sodium
- Fiber: 0 fiber)
- Total Carbohydrate: 71g carbohydrate (70g sugars
- Cholesterol: 0 cholesterol

92. Cranberry Orange Punch

Serving: about 3-1/2 quarts. | Prep: 5mins | Cook: 0mins | Ready in:

Ingredients

- 2 bottles (32 ounces each) cranberry juice, chilled
- 1 cup lemon juice
- 2/3 cup sugar
- 2 cans (12 ounces each) orange soda, chilled
- Ice cubes
- Whole cloves and orange wedges, optional

Direction

- Combine sugar, lemon juice and cranberry juice in several pitchers or a large punch bowl; stir to dissolve the sugar. Right before serving, place in ice and orange soda. Garnish with orange wedges with cloves inserted if preferred.

Nutrition Information

- Calories: 87 calories
- Sodium: 5mg sodium
- Fiber: 0 fiber)
- Total Carbohydrate: 23g carbohydrate (22g sugars
- Cholesterol: 0 cholesterol
- Protein: 0 protein.
- Total Fat: 0 fat (0 saturated fat)

93. Cranberry Pomegranate Margaritas

Serving: 12 servings (3/4 cup each). | Prep: 5mins | Cook: 0mins | Ready in:

Ingredients

- 4-1/2 cups diet lemon-lime soda, chilled
- 1-1/2 cups tequila
- 1-1/2 cups cranberry juice, chilled
- 1-1/2 cups pomegranate juice, chilled
- Pomegranate seeds and frozen cranberries, optional

Direction

- Combine juices, tequila and soda in a pitcher. Pour in chilled glasses to serve. Add cranberries and pomegranate for garnish if preferred.

Nutrition Information

- Calories: 97 calories
- Fiber: 0 fiber)
- Total Carbohydrate: 8g carbohydrate (8g sugars
- Cholesterol: 0 cholesterol
- Protein: 0 protein.
- Total Fat: 0 fat (0 saturated fat)
- Sodium: 13mg sodium

94. Cranberry Punch

Serving: 6 | Prep: 5mins | Cook: | Ready in:

Ingredients

- 1 1/2 liters cranberry-apple juice
- 1 liter ginger ale
- 2 limes, thinly sliced
- 6 sprigs fresh mint
- 6 cups ice

Direction

- Add ice to half-fill 6 tall glasses. Add cranberry-apple juice to fill 3/4 of the glasses. Evenly add ginger ale to the glasses then gently stir. Garnish with mint sprigs and lime.

Nutrition Information

- Calories: 229 calories;
- Sodium: 29
- Total Carbohydrate: 58.4
- Cholesterol: 0
- Protein: 0.5
- Total Fat: 0.1

95. Cranberry Raspberry Punch

Serving: about 5 quarts. | Prep: 10mins | Cook: 0mins | Ready in:

Ingredients

- 2 packages (10 ounces each) frozen sweetened sliced strawberries
- 1 can (12 ounces) frozen lemonade concentrate, thawed
- 1 can (11-1/2 ounces) frozen cranberry raspberry juice concentrate, thawed
- 2 liters ginger ale, chilled
- 2 liters club soda, chilled
- 1 quart raspberry or orange sherbet

Direction

- Combine cranberry raspberry concentrate, lemonade concentrate and strawberries in a blender. Process, covered till smooth. Place into a punch bowl. Add club soda and ginger ale, stir gently. Place scoop of sherbet on top. Serve at once.

Nutrition Information

- Calories: 160 calories
- Total Carbohydrate: 41g carbohydrate (31g sugars
- Cholesterol: 2mg cholesterol
- Protein: 0 protein.
- Total Fat: 1g fat (0 saturated fat)
- Sodium: 45mg sodium
- Fiber: 0 fiber)

96. Cranberry White Sangria

Serving: 24 servings (3/4 cup each). | Prep: 15mins | Cook: 60mins | Ready in:

Ingredients

- 1 large Granny Smith apple, halved and thinly sliced
- 1/2 cup fresh or frozen cranberries
- 1/2 cup whiskey
- 1/4 cup sugar
- 1/4 cup lemon juice
- 1/4 cup lime juice
- 2 bottles (750 milliliters each) sweet white wine
- 1 bottle (750 milliliters) cranberry wine or 3-1/4 cups cranberry juice
- Ice cubes
- 6 cups cold pineapple soda

Direction

- Mix together the first six ingredients in a large pitcher; let sit 30 minutes. Mix in wines. Refrigerate with a cover until cold for at least 30 minutes.
- Fill 1/2 of each glass with ice to serve; put in 1/2 cup wine mixture. Add 1/4 cup pineapple soda on top.

Nutrition Information

- Calories:
- Total Fat:
- Sodium:
- Fiber:
- Total Carbohydrate:
- Cholesterol:
- Protein:

97. Cranberry Banana Smoothies

Serving: 2 servings. | Prep: 5mins | Cook: 0mins | Ready in:

Ingredients

- 1 large banana, peeled, quartered and frozen
- 2/3 cup whole-berry cranberry sauce
- 1/2 cup fat-free vanilla yogurt
- 1/2 cup ice cubes

Direction

- Add in a blender with all ingredients, then cover and blend until smooth. Serve promptly.

Nutrition Information

- Calories: 230 calories
- Protein: 3g protein.
- Total Fat: 0 fat (0 saturated fat)
- Sodium: 21mg sodium
- Fiber: 3g fiber)
- Total Carbohydrate: 56g carbohydrate (35g sugars
- Cholesterol: 2mg cholesterol

98. Cranberry Grape Spritzer

Serving: 1 serving. | Prep: 5mins | Cook: 0mins | Ready in:

Ingredients

- 1/2 cup cranberry-apple juice
- 1/2 cup grape juice
- 1/4 cup club soda
- Lemon slice

Direction

- In a tall glass, combine club soda and juices; place in ice. Add lemon for garnish.

Nutrition Information

- Calories: 134 calories
- Fiber: 0 fiber)
- Total Carbohydrate: 33g carbohydrate (30g sugars
- Cholesterol: 0 cholesterol
- Protein: 1g protein.
- Total Fat: 0 fat (0 saturated fat)
- Sodium: 37mg sodium

99. Cranberry Jalapeno Martini

Serving: 16 servings. | Prep: 30mins | Cook: 0mins | Ready in:

Ingredients

- 1 cup turbinado (washed raw) sugar
- 1-1/2 cups cranberry juice, divided
- 1/2 cup fresh or frozen cranberries
- 1/2 teaspoon chopped seeded jalapeno pepper
- Ice cubes
- 6 cups vodka
- Fresh mint leaves and additional cranberries

Direction

- Combine jalapeno, cranberries, 1/2 cup of cranberry juice and sugar in a large saucepan then boil. Lower the heat then let simmer for 3 minutes, uncovered, to dissolve the sugar. Take away from the heat then cover and allow to stand for 20 minutes.
- Strain and remove jalapeno and cranberries. Cover and store the syrup in the fridge for at least 2 hours to chill.
- To prepare each serving, add ice to fill 3/4 of a tumbler or a mixing glass. Stir in 1 tbsp. of cranberry syrup, 1 tbsp. of cranberry juice and 3 ounces of vodka till it forms condensation on the outside of the glass. In a chilled cocktail glass, strain the drink. Do the process again. Add cranberries and mint for garnish if preferred.

Nutrition Information

- Calories: 252 calories
- Sodium: 1mg sodium
- Fiber: 0 fiber)
- Total Carbohydrate: 15g carbohydrate (15g sugars
- Cholesterol: 0 cholesterol
- Protein: 0 protein.
- Total Fat: 0 fat (0 saturated fat)

100. Cransational Breakfast Drink

Serving: 8 servings. | Prep: 10mins | Cook: 0mins | Ready in:

Ingredients

- 4 cups orange juice
- 2 medium firm bananas, cut into chunks
- 1-1/2 cups frozen cranberries
- 1/4 cup 2% milk
- 1/4 cup sugar
- 4 ice cubes

Direction

- Add ice cubes, sugar, milk, cranberries, bananas and half of the orange juice in a blender, then cover and blend until smooth. Transfer into cold glasses or a pitcher. Do the same process for the leftover ingredients. Serve promptly.

Nutrition Information

- Calories: 121 calories
- Protein: 1g protein. Diabetic Exchanges: 2 fruit.
- Total Fat: 0 fat (0 saturated fat)
- Sodium: 5mg sodium
- Fiber: 2g fiber)

- Total Carbohydrate: 29g carbohydrate (25g sugars
- Cholesterol: 1mg cholesterol

101. Creamy Berry Shakes

Serving: 4 servings. | Prep: 10mins | Cook: 0mins | Ready in:

Ingredients

- 2 cups milk
- 2 cups vanilla ice cream, softened
- 2 cups fresh strawberries
- 1 cup fresh raspberries
- 2 tablespoons sugar
- Whipped topping and additional raspberries, optional

Direction

- Mix the first five ingredients in a blender. Cover the blender and process it for 20 seconds or until smooth. Pour it into the chilled glasses. Garnish the drink with whipped cream and raspberries if you like.

Nutrition Information

- Calories: 268 calories
- Sodium: 113mg sodium
- Fiber: 4g fiber)
- Total Carbohydrate: 36g carbohydrate (28g sugars
- Cholesterol: 46mg cholesterol
- Protein: 7g protein.
- Total Fat: 12g fat (7g saturated fat)

102. Creamy Berry Smoothies

Serving: 2 servings. | Prep: 10mins | Cook: 0mins | Ready in:

Ingredients

- 1/2 cup pomegranate juice
- 1 tablespoon agave syrup or honey
- 3 ounces silken firm tofu (about 1/2 cup)
- 1 cup frozen unsweetened mixed berries
- 1 cup frozen unsweetened strawberries

Direction

- In a blender, add all ingredients then cover and blend until combined. Serve promptly.

Nutrition Information

- Calories: 157 calories
- Fiber: 3g fiber)
- Total Carbohydrate: 35g carbohydrate (29g sugars
- Cholesterol: 0 cholesterol
- Protein: 4g protein.
- Total Fat: 1g fat (0 saturated fat)
- Sodium: 24mg sodium

103. Creamy Holiday Eggnog

Serving: 6 servings (about 4 cups). | Prep: 15mins | Cook: 25mins | Ready in:

Ingredients

- 6 eggs
- 3/4 cup sugar
- 1/4 teaspoon salt
- 4 cups milk, divided
- 1 tablespoon vanilla extract
- 1 teaspoon ground nutmeg
- 1 cup heavy whipping cream
- Additional whipped cream and ground nutmeg, optional

Direction

- Beat the eggs, salt, and sugar in a big saucepan. Slowly add 2 cups of milk.

Constantly stirring, heat on low for 25 minutes, until thermometer says 160°.
- In a big bowl, pour the mixture; then mix in the remaining milk, vanilla, and nutmeg. Put bowl in a bath of ice water; frequently stir until mixture cools down. Blend until smooth in blender if the mixture separates. Put cover on, then chill for 3 or more hours.
- Right before serving, whisk the cream in a little bowl on high speed until soft peaks appear. Slowly mix the whisked cream in with the cooled eggnog. Then pour the mixture in a chilled punch bowl. Serve with nutmeg and scoops of whipped cream on top, if desired.

Nutrition Information

- Calories: 413 calories
- Fiber: 0 fiber)
- Total Carbohydrate: 34g carbohydrate (34g sugars
- Cholesterol: 289mg cholesterol
- Protein: 12g protein.
- Total Fat: 25g fat (14g saturated fat)
- Sodium: 256mg sodium

104. Creamy Lime Coolers

Serving: 2 servings. | Prep: 10mins | Cook: 0mins | Ready in:

Ingredients

- 1 cup unsweetened pineapple juice, chilled
- 1 tablespoon lime juice
- 2 tablespoons confectioners' sugar
- 1/4 teaspoon grated lime zest
- 1 cup vanilla ice cream, softened

Direction

- Combine confectioners' sugar, lime zest, pineapple juice, and lime juice in a blender. Cover the blender and blend the mixture until combined. Add the ice cream. Cover and blend until smooth. Pour the drink into the chilled glasses.

Nutrition Information

- Calories: 234 calories
- Protein: 3g protein.
- Total Fat: 7g fat (4g saturated fat)
- Sodium: 54mg sodium
- Fiber: 0 fiber)
- Total Carbohydrate: 41g carbohydrate (36g sugars
- Cholesterol: 29mg cholesterol

105. Creamy Mandarin Cooler

Serving: 5 servings. | Prep: 5mins | Cook: 0mins | Ready in:

Ingredients

- 3/4 cup fat-free milk
- 1/4 cup orange juice
- 1 can (11 ounces) mandarin oranges, undrained
- 3/4 cup (6 ounces) fat-free reduced-sugar orange creme yogurt
- 1 package (1 ounce) sugar-free instant vanilla pudding mix
- 12 to 15 ice cubes

Direction

- Mix together ice cubes, pudding mix, yogurt, oranges, orange juice and milk in a blender then cover and blend until smooth, about 20 seconds. Stir if needed. Transfer into cold glasses and serve promptly.

Nutrition Information

- Calories: 92 calories
- Sodium: 278mg sodium
- Fiber: 1g fiber)

- Total Carbohydrate: 20g carbohydrate (15g sugars
- Cholesterol: 1mg cholesterol
- Protein: 3g protein. Diabetic Exchanges: 1 fruit
- Total Fat: 0 fat (0 saturated fat)

106. Creamy Mocha Drink

Serving: 4 servings. | Prep: 15mins | Cook: 0mins | Ready in:

Ingredients

- Sugar substitute equivalent to 6 tablespoons sugar
- 2 tablespoons baking cocoa
- 2 tablespoons instant coffee granules
- 1 cup boiling water
- 1 cup 2% milk
- 1/4 teaspoon vanilla extract
- 1-1/2 cups no-sugar-added reduced-fat vanilla ice cream
- 4 tablespoons whipped topping
- 1/4 teaspoon ground cinnamon

Direction

- Combine coffee, cocoa and sugar substitute in a small bowl. Pour in boiling water and stir to dissolve cocoa and coffee. Stir in vanilla and milk. Cover and store in the fridge for at least 1 hour.
- In a blender, place coffee mixture then add ice cream. Cover and blend till smooth. Transfer into glasses or mugs. Add cinnamon and whipped topping for garnish.

Nutrition Information

- Calories: 138 calories
- Cholesterol: 13mg cholesterol
- Protein: 5g protein. Diabetic Exchanges: 1-1/2 starch
- Total Fat: 5g fat (3g saturated fat)
- Sodium: 74mg sodium
- Fiber: 1g fiber)
- Total Carbohydrate: 18g carbohydrate (8g sugars

107. Creamy Orange Drink

Serving: about 6 cups. | Prep: 10mins | Cook: 0mins | Ready in:

Ingredients

- 6 cups orange juice, divided
- 1/2 teaspoon vanilla extract
- 1 package (3.4 ounces) instant vanilla pudding mix
- 1 envelope whipped topping mix (Dream Whip)

Direction

- Mix together pudding and whipped topping mixes, vanilla and 3 cups of orange juice in a small bowl, then beat until smooth. Whisk the leftover orange juice in.
- Transfer into cold glasses and serve promptly.

Nutrition Information

- Calories: 208 calories
- Protein: 1g protein.
- Total Fat: 1g fat (1g saturated fat)
- Sodium: 227mg sodium
- Fiber: 0 fiber)
- Total Carbohydrate: 46g carbohydrate (39g sugars
- Cholesterol: 0 cholesterol

108. Creamy Orange Smoothies

Serving: 12 servings (3/4 cup each). | Prep: 15mins | Cook: 0mins | Ready in:

Ingredients

- 4 cups orange juice
- 3 containers (6 ounces each) orange creme yogurt
- 3 medium bananas, peeled and cut into chunks
- 2 cans (11 ounces each) mandarin oranges, drained
- 6 ounces reduced-fat cream cheese, cubed

Direction

- In a blender, add half of each ingredient, then cover and blend until combined. Place in a big pitcher. Repeat, putting second batch in the same pitcher, then stir to mix. Refrigerate until serving or serve promptly.

Nutrition Information

- Calories: 159 calories
- Protein: 4g protein.
- Total Fat: 4g fat (2g saturated fat)
- Sodium: 85mg sodium
- Fiber: 1g fiber)
- Total Carbohydrate: 29g carbohydrate (24g sugars
- Cholesterol: 12mg cholesterol

109. Creamy Strawberry Breeze

Serving: 4 servings. | Prep: 5mins | Cook: 0mins | Ready in:

Ingredients

- 2 cups whole strawberries
- 2 cups apple juice
- 3 cups whipped topping

Direction

- In a blender, process the apple juice and half of the strawberries until smooth. Add half of the whipped topping and process the mixture again until well-blended. Pour the mixture into the glasses; repeat.

Nutrition Information

- Calories: 230 calories
- Protein: 1g protein.
- Total Fat: 9g fat (9g saturated fat)
- Sodium: 4mg sodium
- Fiber: 2g fiber)
- Total Carbohydrate: 32g carbohydrate (23g sugars
- Cholesterol: 0 cholesterol

110. Creamy Strawberry Punch

Serving: 12-14 servings. | Prep: 15mins | Cook: 0mins | Ready in:

Ingredients

- 4 cups cold milk
- 1 pint strawberry ice cream, softened
- 3/4 cup thawed lemonade concentrate
- 4 cups ginger ale, chilled

Direction

- Mix the ice cream, lemonade concentrate, and milk in a punch bowl or large pitcher until smooth. Whisk in ginger ale. Serve the drink immediately.

Nutrition Information

- Calories: 125 calories
- Sodium: 51mg sodium

- Fiber: 0 fiber)
- Total Carbohydrate: 20g carbohydrate (14g sugars
- Cholesterol: 15mg cholesterol
- Protein: 3g protein.
- Total Fat: 4g fat (2g saturated fat)

111. Cucumber Melon Smoothies

Serving: 6 servings. | Prep: 15mins | Cook: 0mins | Ready in:

Ingredients

- 2 cups reduced-fat plain Greek yogurt
- 1/3 cup honey
- 3 cups chopped honeydew melon
- 2 medium cucumbers, peeled, seeded and chopped
- 1 to 2 tablespoons fresh mint leaves, optional
- 2 cups crushed ice cubes

Direction

- In a blender, place 1/2 of each of these ingredients: mint (if preferred), cucumber, melon, honey and yogurt. Process, covered till blended. Place in 1 cup of ice; cover and blend till smooth. Transfer into 3 glasses. Do the same with the leftover ingredients.

Nutrition Information

- Calories: 155 calories
- Fiber: 2g fiber)
- Total Carbohydrate: 28g carbohydrate (26g sugars
- Cholesterol: 4mg cholesterol
- Protein: 9g protein.
- Total Fat: 2g fat (1g saturated fat)
- Sodium: 48mg sodium

112. Diabetic Milk Shake

Serving: 2 servings. | Prep: 10mins | Cook: 0mins | Ready in:

Ingredients

- 3/4 cup fat-free no-sugar-added vanilla ice cream
- 3/4 cup fat-free milk
- 1 large ripe banana, quartered
- Sugar substitute equivalent to 4 teaspoons sugar
- 1/8 teaspoon vanilla extract

Direction

- In a blender container, combine all the ingredients and process them on low speed until smooth. Serve.

Nutrition Information

- Calories: 162 calories
- Sodium: 99mg sodium
- Fiber: 0 fiber)
- Total Carbohydrate: 29g carbohydrate (0 sugars
- Cholesterol: 9mg cholesterol
- Protein: 6g protein. Diabetic Exchanges: 1 starch
- Total Fat: 3g fat (0 saturated fat)

113. Double Berry Smoothies

Serving: 2 servings. | Prep: 10mins | Cook: 0mins | Ready in:

Ingredients

- 1-1/2 cups sliced fresh strawberries
- 1/2 cup 2% milk
- 1/3 cup blackberry creme yogurt

- 3 to 4 ice cubes

Direction

- In a blender, blend all of the ingredients, covered, till smooth for 1-2 minutes. Transfer into chilled glasses and serve at once.

Nutrition Information

- Calories: 79 calories
- Total Fat: 1g fat (0 saturated fat)
- Sodium: 56mg sodium
- Fiber: 3g fiber)
- Total Carbohydrate: 15g carbohydrate (12g sugars
- Cholesterol: 2mg cholesterol
- Protein: 5g protein. Diabetic Exchanges: 1 fruit.

114. Easy Lemon Lime Punch

Serving: about 3-1/2 quarts. | Prep: 10mins | Cook: 0mins | Ready in:

Ingredients

- 1 envelope (.13 ounce) unsweetened lemon-lime soft drink mix
- 4 cups unsweetened pineapple juice, chilled
- 1 quart lime sherbet
- 2 quarts ginger ale, chilled

Direction

- In a punch bowl, add drink mix, then stir in pineapple juice. Scoop into bowl with sherbet then put in ginger ale and stir lightly. Serve instantly.

Nutrition Information

- Calories: 113 calories
- Cholesterol: 2mg cholesterol
- Protein: 1g protein.
- Total Fat: 1g fat (0 saturated fat)
- Sodium: 25mg sodium
- Fiber: 0 fiber)
- Total Carbohydrate: 27g carbohydrate (25g sugars

115. Effortless Eggnog

Serving: 16 servings (2 quarts). | Prep: 5mins | Cook: 0mins | Ready in:

Ingredients

- 1/2 gallon cold milk, divided
- 1 package (3.4 ounces) instant French vanilla pudding mix
- 1/4 cup sugar
- 2 teaspoons vanilla extract
- 1/2 teaspoon ground cinnamon
- 1/2 teaspoon ground nutmeg

Direction

- Beat pudding mix and 3/4 cup milk in a large bowl until smooth. Whisk in the nutmeg, sugar, cinnamon and vanilla. Add the remaining milk. Store in refrigerator until serving.

Nutrition Information

- Calories: 110 calories
- Protein: 4g protein.
- Total Fat: 4g fat (3g saturated fat)
- Sodium: 144mg sodium
- Fiber: 0 fiber)
- Total Carbohydrate: 14g carbohydrate (13g sugars
- Cholesterol: 17mg cholesterol

116. Eggnog Shakes

Serving: 1-1/2 cups. | Prep: 10mins | Cook: 0mins | Ready in:

Ingredients

- 1-1/2 cups fat-free sugar-free vanilla ice cream
- 1/2 cup fat-free milk
- 1 tablespoon fat-free whipped topping
- Sugar substitute equivalent to 1/2 teaspoon sugar
- 1/8 teaspoon rum extract
- 1/8 teaspoon brandy extract or vanilla extract
- Dash ground nutmeg

Direction

- Combine and blend first six ingredients in a blender. Put cover on and mix until it smoothens. Serve in chilled glasses, and garnish with nutmeg.

Nutrition Information

- Calories: 148 calories
- Fiber: 0 fiber)
- Total Carbohydrate: 30g carbohydrate (11g sugars
- Cholesterol: 1mg cholesterol
- Protein: 8g protein. Diabetic Exchanges: 1-1/2 starch
- Total Fat: 0 fat (0 saturated fat)
- Sodium: 127mg sodium

117. Festive Cranberry Drink

Serving: 3 quarts | Prep: 25mins | Cook: 20mins | Ready in:

Ingredients

- 4 cups fresh or frozen cranberries
- 3 quarts water, divided
- 1-3/4 cups sugar
- 1 cup orange juice
- 2/3 cup lemon juice
- 1/2 cup red-hot candies
- 12 whole cloves

Direction

- Mix 1 qt. water and cranberries in a Dutch oven. Cook until berries pop on medium heat, for 15 minutes. Take away from heat. Use a fine strainer to strain while using a spoon to press the mixture, then get rid of skins. Bring cranberry juice and pulp back to the pan.
- Stir in the leftover water, red-hots, juices and sugar. Put on a double thickness of cheesecloth with cloves. Gather corners of cloth and use a kitchen string to tie to create a bag then put in the juice mixture. Bring to a boil then cook and stir until red-hots and sugar are dissolved.
- Take away from heat then strain through a cheesecloth or a fine mesh sieve. Get rid of the spice bag and serve drink cold or warm.

Nutrition Information

- Calories: 178 calories
- Protein: 0 protein.
- Total Fat: 0 fat (0 saturated fat)
- Sodium: 1mg sodium
- Fiber: 2g fiber)
- Total Carbohydrate: 46g carbohydrate (39g sugars
- Cholesterol: 0 cholesterol

118. Firecracker Mary

Serving: 2 servings. | Prep: 10mins | Cook: 0mins | Ready in:

Ingredients

- 1-1/2 cups tomato juice
- 2 ounces vodka
- 3 tablespoons beef broth

- 2 teaspoons dill pickle juice
- 2 teaspoons stone-ground mustard
- 1 teaspoon lemon juice
- 1 teaspoon lime juice
- 1/2 teaspoon hot pepper sauce
- 1/2 teaspoon Worcestershire sauce
- 1/2 teaspoon prepared horseradish
- 1/4 teaspoon garlic powder
- 1/4 teaspoon pepper
- Ice cubes

Direction

- Mix the initial 12 ingredients in a small pitcher. Pour over ice to serve.

Nutrition Information

- Calories: 109 calories
- Total Carbohydrate: 10g carbohydrate (7g sugars
- Cholesterol: 0 cholesterol
- Protein: 2g protein.
- Total Fat: 1g fat (0 saturated fat)
- Sodium: 743mg sodium
- Fiber: 1g fiber)

119. Four Food Group Shakes

Serving: 2 servings. | Prep: 5mins | Cook: 0mins | Ready in:

Ingredients

- 1/2 cup milk
- 1 cup vanilla ice cream, softened
- 1 medium ripe banana, cut into chunks
- 1 whole graham cracker, broken into large pieces
- 2 tablespoons peanut butter
- 2 tablespoons chocolate syrup
- Cinnamon-sugar, optional

Direction

- Mix the first 6 ingredients in a blender. Cover the blender and process the mixture until smooth. Pour the mixture into the chilled glasses and sprinkle it with cinnamon-sugar if you like. Serve them right away.

Nutrition Information

- Calories: 403 calories
- Total Fat: 19g fat (8g saturated fat)
- Sodium: 215mg sodium
- Fiber: 3g fiber)
- Total Carbohydrate: 53g carbohydrate (39g sugars
- Cholesterol: 37mg cholesterol
- Protein: 10g protein.

120. Four Fruit Drink

Serving: 9 servings. | Prep: 5mins | Cook: 0mins | Ready in:

Ingredients

- 2 cups unsweetened pineapple juice
- 2 cups cranberry juice
- 2 cans (5-1/2 ounces each) apricot nectar
- 1/2 cup lime juice
- 9 lime slices
- 2 cans (12 ounces each) ginger ale, chilled

Direction

- Combine slices of lime, lime juice, apricot nectar, cranberry juice and pineapple juice in a pitcher or a large bowl. Cover then store in the fridge for at least 2 hours. Add in ginger ale and stir right before serving.

Nutrition Information

- Calories: 114 calories
- Total Fat: 0 fat (0 saturated fat)
- Sodium: 12mg sodium

- Fiber: 1g fiber)
- Total Carbohydrate: 30g carbohydrate (26g sugars
- Cholesterol: 0 cholesterol
- Protein: 0 protein. Diabetic Exchanges: 2 fruit.

121.   French Iced Coffee

Serving: 15 servings (3-3/4 quarts). | Prep: 10mins | Cook: 0mins | Ready in:

Ingredients

- 5 cups hot brewed coffee
- 1-1/2 cups sugar
- 6 cups milk
- 3 cups heavy whipping cream
- 1/2 cup chocolate syrup

Direction

- Whisk sugar and coffee in a big bowl till sugar dissolved. Add in the leftover ingredients and stir. Divide into 1–1/2-quart portions and freeze in freezer container overnight.
- Refrigerate till slushy, for 2-3 hours. Immediately serve.

Nutrition Information

- Calories: 328 calories
- Cholesterol: 75mg cholesterol
- Protein: 4g protein.
- Total Fat: 21g fat (13g saturated fat)
- Sodium: 65mg sodium
- Fiber: 0 fiber)
- Total Carbohydrate: 32g carbohydrate (30g sugars

122.   Fresh Lemonade Syrup

Serving: 1 serving. | Prep: 25mins | Cook: 0mins | Ready in:

Ingredients

- 3 cups sugar
- 1 cup boiling water
- 3 cups lemon juice (about 16 lemons)
- 2 tablespoon grated lemon zest

Direction

- Add boiling water and sugar in a 1 1/2-qt heatproof container to dissolve sugar well. Let it cool. Put in the lemon zest and juice then mix thoroughly. Cover it and keep in the fridge for maximum of 7 days. This recipe yield about 5 1/2 cup syrup (the concentration of lemonade determines the number of batches.
- Preparing lemonade: Mix 3/4 cup cold water and 1/4 to 1/3 cup syrup in a glass for each serving, then stir well. Mix 5 cups cold water and 2 2/3 cups syrup in a 2-quarter pitcher to make 8 servings, then stir well.

Nutrition Information

- Calories: 126 calories
- Sodium: 1mg sodium
- Fiber: 0 fiber)
- Total Carbohydrate: 33g carbohydrate (30g sugars
- Cholesterol: 0 cholesterol
- Protein: 0 protein.
- Total Fat: 0 fat (0 saturated fat)

123.   Fresh Squeezed Pink Lemonade

Serving: 6 servings. | Prep: 5mins | Cook: 10mins | Ready in:

Ingredients

- 4 cups water, divided
- 1 cup sugar
- 3 lemon peel strips
- 1 cup lemon juice (about 5 lemons)
- 1 tablespoon grape juice
- Lemon slices and maraschino cherries, optional

Direction

- Add lemon peel, sugar and 2 cups water in a small saucepan and bring the mixture to a boil. Lower heat and simmer for 5 minutes with a cover. Take away from heat then get rid of the lemon peel.
- Mix the sugar mixture, grape juice, lemon juice and remaining water in a big pitcher. Serve over ice and decorate with lemon slices and cherries if you want.

Nutrition Information

- Calories: 141 calories
- Sodium: 1mg sodium
- Fiber: 0 fiber)
- Total Carbohydrate: 37g carbohydrate (35g sugars
- Cholesterol: 0 cholesterol
- Protein: 0 protein.
- Total Fat: 0 fat (0 saturated fat)

124. Frosty Chocolate Raspberry Latte

Serving: 4 servings. | Prep: 5mins | Cook: 0mins | Ready in:

Ingredients

- 1/2 cup hot water
- 1 tablespoon instant espresso powder
- 1-1/4 cup lowfat milk
- 3 tablespoons chocolate syrup
- 1 package (10 oz.) frozen raspberries in syrup, broken in chunks
- 2-1/2 cups light vanilla ice cream
- Aerosol whipped cream
- Chocolate syrup, for decoration

Direction

- In a blender jar, add espresso powder and water. Allow to stand for 30 seconds. Place in raspberries, chocolate syrup and milk.
- Cover; use SMOOTHIE button to blend for about 10 seconds. Put ice cream in the blender jar. Cover then blend on HIGH till incorporated and smooth. If necessary, scrape the blender jar's sides.
- Transfer into tall and thin glasses. Add a sprinkle of chocolate syrup and a shot of whipped cream to garnish. Add a straw to serve.

Nutrition Information

- Calories:
- Total Fat:
- Sodium:
- Fiber:
- Total Carbohydrate:
- Cholesterol:
- Protein:

125. Frosty Fruit Drink

Serving: 4 servings. | Prep: 10mins | Cook: 0mins | Ready in:

Ingredients

- 1 cup unsweetened raspberries
- 2 medium ripe bananas
- 1-1/2 cups frozen vanilla yogurt
- 1-1/2 cups raspberry-blend juice, chilled

Direction

- Combine all the ingredients in a blender. Cover the blender and process the mixture until smooth. Pour it into the glasses to serve.

Nutrition Information

- Calories: 206 calories
- Total Carbohydrate: 40g carbohydrate (35g sugars
- Cholesterol: 9mg cholesterol
- Protein: 5g protein.
- Total Fat: 3g fat (2g saturated fat)
- Sodium: 64mg sodium
- Fiber: 2g fiber)

126. Frosty Fruit Slush

Serving: 24 servings. | Prep: 10mins | Cook: 0mins | Ready in:

Ingredients

- 2 cans (8 ounces each) crushed pineapple, drained
- 1 can (11 ounces) mandarin oranges, drained
- 5 large ripe bananas, sliced
- 2 cups sliced fresh strawberries
- 2 cups water
- 1 can (12 ounces) frozen lemonade concentrate, thawed
- 1 can (12 ounces) frozen orange juice concentrate, thawed
- 1 cup diet lemon-lime soda

Direction

- Put strawberries, bananas, oranges and half of a pineapple in a blender. Cover and blend until smooth. Transfer into a big bowl. Repeat. Whisk in the leftover ingredients. Scoop or pour into each of 24 plastic cups or glasses with 1/2 cup mixture. Cover and freeze for minimum of 2 hours.
- Before serving, take out of the freezer about 15 minutes. It can be frozen for maximum of 1 month.

Nutrition Information

- Calories: 95 calories
- Total Fat: 1g fat (0 saturated fat)
- Sodium: 4mg sodium
- Fiber: 1g fiber)
- Total Carbohydrate: 24g carbohydrate (0 sugars
- Cholesterol: 0 cholesterol
- Protein: 1g protein. Diabetic Exchanges: 1-1/2 fruit.

127. Frosty Lemon Drink

Serving: 4 servings. | Prep: 10mins | Cook: 0mins | Ready in:

Ingredients

- 3/4 cup cold water
- 3/4 cup thawed lemonade concentrate
- 1/2 cup nonfat dry milk powder
- 1/3 cup sugar
- 1/8 teaspoon almond extract
- 16 to 18 ice cubes

Direction

- Mix the first 5 ingredients in a blender. Cover and blend on high speed until combined. A few at a time, add in ice cubes. Cover and blend until get slushy texture. Transfer into cold glasses and serve promptly.

Nutrition Information

- Calories: 219 calories
- Sodium: 84mg sodium
- Fiber: 0 fiber)

- Total Carbohydrate: 50g carbohydrate (47g sugars
- Cholesterol: 3mg cholesterol
- Protein: 6g protein.
- Total Fat: 0 fat (0 saturated fat)

128. Frosty Mocha Drink

Serving: 4 servings. | Prep: 15mins | Cook: 0mins | Ready in:

Ingredients

- 1 cup milk
- 3 tablespoons instant chocolate drink mix
- 2 tablespoons instant coffee granules
- 2 tablespoons honey
- 1 teaspoon vanilla extract
- 14 to 16 ice cubes

Direction

- Combine all the ingredients in a blender. Cover and process the mixture until smooth. Pour it into the chilled glasses to serve.

Nutrition Information

- Calories: 143 calories
- Protein: 3g protein.
- Total Fat: 3g fat (2g saturated fat)
- Sodium: 72mg sodium
- Fiber: 1g fiber)
- Total Carbohydrate: 30g carbohydrate (27g sugars
- Cholesterol: 8mg cholesterol

129. Frosty Orange Smoothie

Serving: 4-5 servings. | Prep: 10mins | Cook: 0mins | Ready in:

Ingredients

- 1 can (6 ounces) frozen orange juice concentrate, thawed
- 1 cup milk
- 1 cup water
- 1/4 cup sugar
- 1 teaspoon vanilla extract
- 10 to 12 ice cubes

Direction

- Mix vanilla, sugar, water, milk and orange juice in a blender then cover and blend until smooth. One at a time, put in ice cubes through the hole of the lid while blender running, blend until smooth. Serve promptly.

Nutrition Information

- Calories: 156 calories
- Cholesterol: 8mg cholesterol
- Protein: 3g protein.
- Total Fat: 2g fat (1g saturated fat)
- Sodium: 31mg sodium
- Fiber: 0 fiber)
- Total Carbohydrate: 32g carbohydrate (31g sugars

130. Frosty's Fruit Slush

Serving: 10-12 servings. | Prep: 10mins | Cook: 0mins | Ready in:

Ingredients

- 2 cups frozen peach slices
- 2 cans (5-1/2 ounces each) apricot or peach nectar
- 1 can (6 ounces) frozen orange juice concentrate, thawed
- 2 liters lemon-lime soda, chilled

Direction

- Combine orange juice, nectar and peaches in a blender. Cover and blend till smooth. Transfer into ice cube trays. Let freeze till firm, for 3-4 hours. Before serving, take away from the freezer for 30 minutes. Add 2-3 cubes into each glass for each serving. Pour in soda and stir till cubes dissolve.

Nutrition Information

- Calories: 117 calories
- Total Carbohydrate: 30g carbohydrate (29g sugars
- Cholesterol: 0 cholesterol
- Protein: 1g protein.
- Total Fat: 0 fat (0 saturated fat)
- Sodium: 20mg sodium
- Fiber: 1g fiber)

131. Frothy Orange Drink

Serving: 4 cups. | Prep: 10mins | Cook: 0mins | Ready in:

Ingredients

- 1 cup water
- 1 cup milk
- 1 can (6 ounces) frozen orange juice concentrate, thawed
- 1/2 cup sugar
- 1 teaspoon vanilla extract
- 8 to 10 ice cubes

Direction

- Mix all ingredients in a blender, then cover and blend until slushy and thickened. Transfer into cold glasses and serve promptly.

Nutrition Information

- Calories: 204 calories
- Sodium: 32mg sodium
- Fiber: 0 fiber)
- Total Carbohydrate: 44g carbohydrate (43g sugars
- Cholesterol: 8mg cholesterol
- Protein: 3g protein.
- Total Fat: 2g fat (1g saturated fat)

132. Frothy Orange Pineapple Cooler

Serving: 6 servings. | Prep: 5mins | Cook: 0mins | Ready in:

Ingredients

- 2 cups unsweetened pineapple juice
- 1 cup (8 ounces) vanilla yogurt
- 1 can (6 ounces) frozen orange juice concentrate, thawed
- 2 small ripe bananas, cut into chunks
- 1/2 cup frozen unsweetened strawberries
- 1 drop coconut extract, optional

Direction

- Mix all ingredients in a blender, then cover and process on high until smooth. Transfer into cold glasses and serve promptly.

Nutrition Information

- Calories: 168 calories
- Sodium: 29mg sodium
- Fiber: 1g fiber)
- Total Carbohydrate: 37g carbohydrate (35g sugars
- Cholesterol: 4mg cholesterol
- Protein: 3g protein.
- Total Fat: 2g fat (1g saturated fat)

133. Frozen Hot Chocolate

Serving: 2 | Prep: 5mins | Cook: | Ready in:

Ingredients

- 1 cup crushed ice
- 1 cup milk
- 1 (1 ounce) envelope instant hot chocolate mix

Direction

- In a blender, blend together hot chocolate mix, milk and ice until smooth.

Nutrition Information

- Calories: 117 calories;
- Sodium: 124
- Total Carbohydrate: 17.4
- Cholesterol: 10
- Protein: 5
- Total Fat: 3

134. Frozen Rhubarb Slush

Serving: 22 servings (1 cup each). | Prep: 30mins | Cook: 10mins | Ready in:

Ingredients

- 8 cups diced fresh or frozen rhubarb
- 1 package (16 ounces) frozen unsweetened strawberries
- 3 cups sugar
- 8 cups water
- 1 package (3 ounces) strawberry gelatin
- 1/2 cup lemon juice
- 11 cups ginger ale, chilled
- Rhubarb curls, optional

Direction

- Bring the water, sugar, strawberries and rhubarb to a boil in a Dutch oven. Lower heat and simmer until rhubarb is softened, without a cover, about 5 to 8 minutes. Strain through a sieve, discard pulp. Stir in lemon juice and gelatin until dissolved.
- Turn the mixture to a freezer container and freeze until solid, stirring sometimes. It can be frozen for up to 3 months.
- When ready to use: Mix even amounts of ginger ale and rhubarb mixture in several pitchers or a punch bowl. For each serving, mix in a glass with 1/2 cup ginger ale and 1/2 cup rhubarb mixture. Decorate with rhubarb curls if you want. Serve promptly.

Nutrition Information

- Calories: 179 calories
- Cholesterol: 0 cholesterol
- Protein: 1g protein.
- Total Fat: 0 fat (0 saturated fat)
- Sodium: 20mg sodium
- Fiber: 1g fiber)
- Total Carbohydrate: 46g carbohydrate (43g sugars

135. Frozen Strawberry Daiquiris

Serving: 4 servings. | Prep: 10mins | Cook: 0mins | Ready in:

Ingredients

- 3/4 cup rum
- 1/2 cup thawed limeade concentrate
- 1 package (10 ounces) frozen sweetened sliced strawberries
- 1 to 1-1/2 cups ice cubes
- GARNISH:
- Fresh strawberries

Direction

- Combine ice, strawberries, limeade concentrate and rum in a blender. Cover and blend till thick and smooth. If you want thicker daiquiris, add more ice. Transfer into cocktail glasses.

- For garnish each daiquiri: Make a 1/2-inch slit on the tip of a strawberry and place berry on the rim of each glass.

Nutrition Information

- Calories: 232 calories
- Fiber: 1g fiber)
- Total Carbohydrate: 36g carbohydrate (31g sugars
- Cholesterol: 0 cholesterol
- Protein: 0 protein.
- Total Fat: 0 fat (0 saturated fat)
- Sodium: 3mg sodium

136. Fruit Juice Cooler

Serving: 4 | Prep: 2mins | Cook: |Ready in:

Ingredients

- 1½ cups peach nectar, chilled
- ½ cup orange juice, chilled
- ¼ cup grapefruit juice, chilled
- 1 tablespoon lemon juice
- 1½ cups sparkling mineral water, chilled
- Ice cubes
- Star fruit slices (optional)

Direction

- Stir lemon juice, grapefruit juice, orange juice and peach nectar together in a pitcher.
- Gradually add in mineral water and stir. Pour over ice to serve. Add a slice of star fruit if preferred.

Nutrition Information

- Calories: 71 calories;
- Protein: 1
- Total Fat: 0
- Saturated Fat: 0
- Sodium: 8
- Fiber: 1
- Total Carbohydrate: 18
- Cholesterol: 0

137. Fruit Punch

Serving: 60 | Prep: 5mins | Cook: |Ready in:

Ingredients

- 1 (64 fluid ounce) bottle fruit punch, chilled
- 1 (64 fluid ounce) bottle unsweetened pineapple juice, chilled
- 1 (2 liter) bottle ginger ale, chilled
- 1/2 gallon orange sherbet

Direction

- Mix ginger ale, pineapple juice and fruit punch together in a punch bowl. Put scoops off sherbet into the punch. Wait for approximately 10 minutes, when the sherbet starts to melt, stir gently to serve.

Nutrition Information

- Calories: 43 calories;
- Total Fat: 0
- Sodium: 16
- Total Carbohydrate: 10.6
- Cholesterol: 0
- Protein: 0.1

138. Fruit Smoothies

Serving: 3 servings. | Prep: 5mins | Cook: 0mins |Ready in:

Ingredients

- 3/4 cup fat-free milk
- 1/2 cup orange juice

- 1/2 cup unsweetened applesauce
- 1 small ripe banana, halved
- 1/2 cup frozen unsweetened raspberries
- 7 to 10 ice cubes

Direction

- Combine all of the ingredients in a blender. Cover and blend till smooth. Transfer into chilled glasses and serve at once.

Nutrition Information

- Calories: 97 calories
- Total Fat: 0 fat (0 saturated fat)
- Sodium: 33mg sodium
- Fiber: 2g fiber)
- Total Carbohydrate: 22g carbohydrate (18g sugars
- Cholesterol: 1mg cholesterol
- Protein: 3g protein. Diabetic Exchanges: 1-1/2 fruit.

139. Fruited Punch

Serving: 24 servings (3/4 cup each). | Prep: 10mins | Cook: 10mins | Ready in:

Ingredients

- 1-1/2 cups sugar
- 1-1/2 cups water
- 1 bottle (2 liters) ginger ale, chilled
- 3 cups strong brewed tea, chilled
- 3 cups cold orange juice
- 3 cups cold unsweetened pineapple juice
- 1/2 cup lemon juice
- 3 cups thinly sliced fresh strawberries or frozen unsweetened sliced strawberries

Direction

- To make sugar syrup, combine water and sugar in a small saucepan then let boil over medium heat. Lower heat and let simmer for 3-4 minutes, uncovered, stir occasionally to dissolve the sugar. Let cool completely. Pour into a covered container and store in the fridge for 1 hour till cold.
- For serving, in a punch bowl, combine sugar syrup, fruit juices, tea and ginger ale. Or, place the ingredients into 2 pitchers and stir till combined. Add strawberries to serve.

Nutrition Information

- Calories: 107 calories
- Sodium: 7mg sodium
- Fiber: 0 fiber)
- Total Carbohydrate: 27g carbohydrate (25g sugars
- Cholesterol: 0 cholesterol
- Protein: 0 protein.
- Total Fat: 0 fat (0 saturated fat)

140. Fruity Breakfast Beverage

Serving: 3-4 servings (3-1/2 cups). | Prep: 10mins | Cook: 0mins | Ready in:

Ingredients

- 2 cups orange juice
- 1 frozen banana, quartered
- 1/2 cup unsweetened frozen strawberries
- 1/2 cup unsweetened frozen raspberries
- 1 teaspoon honey

Direction

- In a blender, combine all of the ingredients till smooth.

Nutrition Information

- Calories: 135 calories
- Cholesterol: 0 cholesterol
- Protein: 1g protein.
- Total Fat: 0 fat (0 saturated fat)

- Sodium: 1mg sodium
- Fiber: 2g fiber)
- Total Carbohydrate: 33g carbohydrate (27g sugars

141. Fruity Lemonade

Serving: 8 servings, about 1-1/4 cups each | Prep: 10mins | Cook: | Ready in:

Ingredients

- 1 bottle (2 L) carbonated lemon-lime soda, chilled
- 1/2 cup COUNTRY TIME Lemonade Flavor Drink Mix
- 2 cups chopped mixed fruit (cherries, kiwi, melon and strawberries)

Direction

- 1. In a 2-qt glass or plastic pitcher with drink mix inside, put in soda till mix is totally melt.
- 2. Scoop in each of 8 glasses with 1/4 cup fruit.
- 3. Pour in prepared drink.

Nutrition Information

- Calories: 150
- Sodium: 35 mg
- Sugar: 36 g
- Protein: 0 g
- Total Fat: 0 g
- Saturated Fat: 0 g
- Fiber: 1 g
- Total Carbohydrate: 37 g
- Cholesterol: 0 mg

142. Fruity Milk Shakes

Serving: about 4 cups. | Prep: 15mins | Cook: 0mins | Ready in:

Ingredients

- 3/4 cup thawed apple juice concentrate
- 1 cup (8 ounces) vanilla yogurt
- 1 medium ripe banana, sliced
- 1/2 cup nonfat dry milk powder
- 1/4 teaspoon coconut extract
- 1 to 3 teaspoons honey
- 12 ice cubes

Direction

- Mix the first five ingredients in a blender. Cover and process until it is well-combined. Add the ice and honey. Cover again and process on High setting until the mixture is foamy and the ice is crushed. Pour it into the glasses.

Nutrition Information

- Calories: 216 calories
- Sodium: 128mg sodium
- Fiber: 1g fiber)
- Total Carbohydrate: 41g carbohydrate (39g sugars
- Cholesterol: 9mg cholesterol
- Protein: 9g protein.
- Total Fat: 2g fat (1g saturated fat)

143. Fruity Mint Punch

Serving: 4-1/2 quarts. | Prep: 15mins | Cook: 0mins | Ready in:

Ingredients

- 8 individual tea bags
- 1/2 to 3/4 cup minced fresh mint
- 4 cups boiling water
- 1-1/2 cups sugar
- 3/4 cup thawed lemonade concentrate
- 3/4 cup thawed limeade concentrate
- 3/4 cup orange juice
- 3 quarts cold water

Direction

- In a heat-resistant bowl or pitcher, place mint and tea bags. Pour in boiling water. Allow to stand for 5 minutes then strain. Add orange juice, concentrates and sugar; stir then store in the fridge.
- Right before serving, into a large punch bowl, add the mint mixture then add cold water and stir.

Nutrition Information

- Calories: 114 calories
- Protein: 0 protein.
- Total Fat: 0 fat (0 saturated fat)
- Sodium: 1mg sodium
- Fiber: 0 fiber)
- Total Carbohydrate: 30g carbohydrate (27g sugars
- Cholesterol: 0 cholesterol

144. Fruity Punch

Serving: about 1 quart. | Prep: 15mins | Cook: 0mins | Ready in:

Ingredients

- 2-1/2 cups unsweetened pineapple juice
- 1 cup ginger ale, chilled
- 1 cup vanilla ice cream, softened
- 1 cup orange sherbet

Direction

- Combine ginger ale and pineapple juice in a small punch bowl. Place scoops of sherbet and ice cream on top. Serve the punch at once.

Nutrition Information

- Calories: 226 calories
- Fiber: 0 fiber)
- Total Carbohydrate: 46g carbohydrate (41g sugars
- Cholesterol: 17mg cholesterol
- Protein: 2g protein.
- Total Fat: 4g fat (3g saturated fat)
- Sodium: 49mg sodium

145. Fruity Slush

Serving: 13 servings (about 2 quarts). | Prep: 10mins | Cook: 0mins | Ready in:

Ingredients

- 1 package (3 ounces) raspberry gelatin
- 1 cup boiling water
- 2 cups cold water
- 2 cups cranberry juice
- 1 can (12 ounces) frozen pink lemonade concentrate, thawed
- 1 can (12 ounces) frozen orange juice concentrate, thawed
- 1 liter lemon-lime soda, chilled

Direction

- Let gelatin dissolve in a large bowl of boiling water. Stir in concentrates, cranberry juice and cold water. Transfer into a 2 1/2-qt. freezer container. Cover and store the container in freezer overnight.
- 2 hours before serving, take the container out of the freezer. Add slush to fill 2/3 of the glasses then stir into each glass with 1 cup of soda.

Nutrition Information

- Calories: 102 calories
- Sodium: 14mg sodium
- Fiber: 0 fiber)
- Total Carbohydrate: 26g carbohydrate (0 sugars
- Cholesterol: 0 cholesterol

- Protein: 1g protein. Diabetic Exchanges: 1-1/2 fruit.
- Total Fat: 0 fat (0 saturated fat)

146. Fruity Summer Cooler

Serving: 2-3 servings. | Prep: 10mins | Cook: 0mins | Ready in:

Ingredients

- 6 to 8 ice cubes
- 1/2 cup cubed cantaloupe
- 1/2 cup pineapple chunks
- 1/2 cup cranberry juice
- 1/3 cup sliced banana
- 1/4 cup pineapple juice
- 1 tablespoon honey
- 3/4 teaspoon lemon juice
- 1/4 teaspoon grated lemon zest

Direction

- Mix all ingredients together in a blender then cover and blend until smooth. Transfer into cold glasses and serve promptly.

Nutrition Information

- Calories: 102 calories
- Sodium: 4mg sodium
- Fiber: 1g fiber)
- Total Carbohydrate: 27g carbohydrate (24g sugars
- Cholesterol: 0 cholesterol
- Protein: 1g protein. Diabetic Exchanges: 1-1/2 fruit.
- Total Fat: 0 fat (0 saturated fat)

147. Ginger Ale Fruit Punch

Serving: 3 quarts. | Prep: 5mins | Cook: 0mins | Ready in:

Ingredients

- 1 quart white grape juice, chilled
- 1 quart cranberry-raspberry juice, chilled
- 1 liter ginger ale, chilled

Direction

- Mix all ingredients together in a big pitcher or punch bowl, then serve promptly.

Nutrition Information

- Calories: 118 calories
- Cholesterol: 0 cholesterol
- Protein: 0 protein.
- Total Fat: 0 fat (0 saturated fat)
- Sodium: 14mg sodium
- Fiber: 0 fiber)
- Total Carbohydrate: 29g carbohydrate (28g sugars

148. Ginger Ale Mock Champagne

Serving: 16 servings. | Prep: 10mins | Cook: 0mins | Ready in:

Ingredients

- 3 cups apple cider or juice
- 3 cups unsweetened pineapple juice
- 3/4 cup frozen lemonade concentrate, thawed
- 1/4 cup sugar
- 2 liters ginger ale, chilled

Direction

- Mix together sugar, lemonade concentrate, pineapple juice and apple cider in a 2 1/2-qt.

freezer container, then cover and put in the freezer overnight. Before serving, take out of the freezer and allow to stand at room temperature about 2 hours.
- Right before serving, use a wooden spoon to break up the mixture then turn to a punch bowl. Whisk in the ginger ale.

Nutrition Information

- Calories:
- Protein:
- Total Fat:
- Sodium:
- Fiber:
- Total Carbohydrate:
- Cholesterol:

149. Ginger Apple Fizz

Serving: 2 servings. | Prep: 5mins | Cook: 0mins | Ready in:

Ingredients

- 1/4 cup thawed apple juice concentrate
- 1/8 teaspoon ground ginger
- 2 cups chilled club soda
- Ice cubes

Direction

- Combine ginger and apple juice concentrate in a pitcher. Gradually add in soda and stir. Pour over ice in chilled glasses to serve.

Nutrition Information

- Calories: 59 calories
- Fiber: 0 fiber)
- Total Carbohydrate: 15g carbohydrate (0 sugars
- Cholesterol: 0 cholesterol
- Protein: 0 protein. Diabetic Exchanges: 1 fruit.
- Total Fat: 0 fat (0 saturated fat)
- Sodium: 59mg sodium

150. Ginger Peach Smoothies

Serving: 2 servings. | Prep: 5mins | Cook: 0mins | Ready in:

Ingredients

- 2 cups frozen unsweetened sliced peaches
- 1 cup reduced-fat plain yogurt
- 1/2 cup apricot nectar
- 1/4 cup ginger ale, chilled
- 2 tablespoons honey
- 1/8 to 1/4 teaspoon minced fresh gingerroot

Direction

- Mix all ingredients in a blender, then cover and blend until combined. Transfer into cold glasses and serve promptly.

Nutrition Information

- Calories: 253 calories
- Sodium: 91mg sodium
- Fiber: 3g fiber)
- Total Carbohydrate: 54g carbohydrate (51g sugars
- Cholesterol: 7mg cholesterol
- Protein: 8g protein.
- Total Fat: 2g fat (1g saturated fat)

151. Ginger Kale Smoothies

Serving: 2 servings. | Prep: 15mins | Cook: 0mins | Ready in:

Ingredients

- 1-1/4 cups orange juice

- 1 teaspoon lemon juice
- 2 cups torn fresh kale
- 1 medium apple, peeled and coarsely chopped
- 1 tablespoon minced fresh gingerroot
- 4 ice cubes
- 1/8 teaspoon ground cinnamon
- 1/8 teaspoon ground turmeric or 1/4-inch piece fresh turmeric, peeled and finely chopped
- Dash cayenne pepper

Direction

- In a blender, add all ingredients then cover and blend until combined. Serve promptly.

Nutrition Information

- Calories: 121 calories
- Cholesterol: 0 cholesterol
- Protein: 1g protein. Diabetic Exchanges: 1-1/2 fruit
- Total Fat: 0 fat (0 saturated fat)
- Sodium: 22mg sodium
- Fiber: 2g fiber
- Total Carbohydrate: 29g carbohydrate (21g sugars

152. Golden Fruit Punch With Ice Ring

Serving: 21 servings (4 quarts). | Prep: 10mins | Cook: 0mins | Ready in:

Ingredients

- 4 maraschino cherries
- 1 medium navel orange, thinly sliced
- 1 small lemon, thinly sliced
- 1 small lime, thinly sliced
- 1 can (12 ounces) frozen lemonade concentrate, thawed
- 1 can (12 ounces) frozen limeade concentrate, thawed
- 1 can (12 ounces) frozen pineapple-orange juice concentrate, thawed
- 2 liters diet ginger ale, chilled

Direction

- In a ring mold with 5 cups, place fruit and add 3/4 cup of water. Store in the freezer till solid. Fill the mold with enough water then let freeze till solid.
- Combine 2 cups of water with juice concentrates in a punch bowl right before serving. Add in ginger ale and stir. Use a hot damp dishcloth to wrap the mold's bottom and unmold ice ring. Invert and place onto a baking sheet. Transfer into the punch bowl with the fruit side facing up.

Nutrition Information

- Calories: 96 calories
- Sodium: 22mg sodium
- Fiber: 0 fiber
- Total Carbohydrate: 24g carbohydrate (21g sugars
- Cholesterol: 0 cholesterol
- Protein: 0 protein. Diabetic Exchanges: 1 starch
- Total Fat: 0 fat (0 saturated fat)

153. Golden Smoothies

Serving: 3 cups. | Prep: 10mins | Cook: 0mins | Ready in:

Ingredients

- 1-1/2 cups orange juice
- 1 cup (8 ounces) peach yogurt
- 1 can (5-1/2 ounces) apricot nectar
- 1 teaspoon honey
- Orange slices and maraschino cherries, optional

Direction

- In a blender, add first 4 ingredient, then cover and blend until smooth. Transfer into glasses and decorate with cherries and oranges, if you want.

Nutrition Information

- Calories: 128 calories
- Total Carbohydrate: 29g carbohydrate (0 sugars
- Cholesterol: 2mg cholesterol
- Protein: 3g protein. Diabetic Exchanges: 1 fruit
- Total Fat: 0 fat (0 saturated fat)
- Sodium: 37mg sodium
- Fiber: 0 fiber)

154. Grape Juice Sparkler

Serving: 10 servings (2 quarts). | Prep: 15mins | Cook: 0mins |Ready in:

Ingredients

- 1 can (11-1/2 ounces) frozen cranberry-raspberry juice concentrate, thawed
- 1 bottle (1 liter) club soda, chilled
- 1 bottle (750 ml) sparkling white grape juice, chilled
- 20 to 30 fresh raspberries

Direction

- Before you serve, in a large pitcher, mix the juice concentrate with club soda. Mix in the sparkling grape juice. Put 2 to 3 raspberries on the bottom of every glass. Pour in juice.

Nutrition Information

- Calories: 111 calories
- Protein: 0 protein. Diabetic Exchanges: 2 fruit.
- Total Fat: 0 fat (0 saturated fat)
- Sodium: 28mg sodium
- Fiber: 0 fiber)
- Total Carbohydrate: 30g carbohydrate (15g sugars
- Cholesterol: 0 cholesterol

155. Grape Punch

Serving: 18 (1/2-cup) servings. | Prep: 5mins | Cook: 0mins |Ready in:

Ingredients

- 2 cups red grape juice, chilled
- 2 cups white grape juice, chilled
- 5 cups lemon-lime soda, chilled

Direction

- Combine the juices in a pitcher or a large punch bowl then mix well. Just before serving, pour in soda and stir.

Nutrition Information

- Calories: 60 calories
- Sodium: 11mg sodium
- Fiber: 0 fiber)
- Total Carbohydrate: 15g carbohydrate (14g sugars
- Cholesterol: 0 cholesterol
- Protein: 0 protein.
- Total Fat: 0 fat (0 saturated fat)

156. Grasshopper Shakes

Serving: 10 servings (2-1/2 quarts). | Prep: 10mins | Cook: 0mins |Ready in:

Ingredients

- 2 quarts vanilla ice cream
- 1 carton (8 ounces) frozen whipped topping, thawed

- 3/4 cup green creme de menthe
- 3/4 cup creme de cacao

Direction

- Cover and process the ingredients in batches in a blender till blended. Stir if needed. Transfer into chilled glasses and serve at once.

Nutrition Information

- Calories: 425 calories
- Fiber: 0 fiber)
- Total Carbohydrate: 47g carbohydrate (38g sugars
- Cholesterol: 46mg cholesterol
- Protein: 4g protein.
- Total Fat: 16g fat (11g saturated fat)
- Sodium: 86mg sodium

157. Grilled Lemon & Thyme Lemonade

Serving: 9 servings (1 cup each). | Prep: 25mins | Cook: 5mins | Ready in:

Ingredients

- 15 fresh thyme sprigs
- 2 cups water, divided
- 1 cup sugar, divided
- 9 medium lemons, halved
- 1/4 cup honey
- 1/4 teaspoon almond extract
- 5 cups cold water

Direction

- Steep thyme sprigs in a small bowl with 1 cup water, at the same time, prepare lemons. On a plate, put in 1/4 cup sugar. Plunge the lemon's cut sides in sugar.
- Cover and grill lemon for 1 to 2 minutes on medium high heat with cut side down, until turns golden brown color. Let cool a little bit. Drain thyme and grill for 1 to 2 minutes while flipping one time, until has slight brown color.
- Mix the leftover sugar, honey and 1 cup water in a small saucepan then bring the mixture to a boil while stirring continuously to dissolve sugar. Take away from heat. Put in grilled thyme sprigs and extract. Allow it to stand for an hour to soak. Get rid of the thyme.
- At the same time, squeeze lemons to extract 1 1/2 cups juice then strain. Mix together lemon juice, thyme syrup and 5 cups cold water in a big pitcher. Serve over ice.

Nutrition Information

- Calories:
- Total Fat:
- Sodium:
- Fiber:
- Total Carbohydrate:
- Cholesterol:
- Protein:

158. Grinch Punch

Serving: 4 quarts. | Prep: 15mins | Cook: 5mins | Ready in:

Ingredients

- 1/3 cup sugar
- 3 tablespoons water
- 1/3 cup evaporated milk
- 1/2 teaspoon almond extract
- 12 drops neon green food coloring
- 1 bottle (2 liters) lemon-lime soda, chilled
- 2 pints vanilla ice cream

Direction

- Combine water and sugar in a large saucepan. Over medium heat, cook and stir to dissolve the sugar then take away from the heat. Stir in extract and milk. Place in a bowl and let cool

- to room temperature. Cover and store in the fridge to chill.
- Place the milk mixture into a punch bowl right before serving. Add in soda and food coloring; stir. Place scoops of ice cream on top.

Nutrition Information

- Calories: 142 calories
- Sodium: 46mg sodium
- Fiber: 0 fiber)
- Total Carbohydrate: 26g carbohydrate (24g sugars
- Cholesterol: 16mg cholesterol
- Protein: 1g protein.
- Total Fat: 4g fat (2g saturated fat)

159. Gummy Worm Punch

Serving: 3 quarts. | Prep: 15mins | Cook: 0mins | Ready in:

Ingredients

- 4 cups unsweetened apple juice
- 4 cups orange juice
- 2/3 cup thawed lemonade concentrate
- 2 cups water
- 20 gummy worms
- 4 cups lemon-lime soda, chilled

Direction

- Combine the lemonade concentrate, orange juice, and apple juice in a punch bowl. Pour 1 cup of the juice mixture and water into a 5-cup ring mold; put in the gummy worms. Then freeze until solid. In the meantime, freeze the juice mixture until chilled.
- Add soda to the juice mixture prior to serving. In a damp hot dishcloth, wrap the mold's bottom to unmold the ice ring; invert onto a baking sheet. Arrange in the punch bowl with the worm side up.

Nutrition Information

- Calories:
- Protein:
- Total Fat:
- Sodium:
- Fiber:
- Total Carbohydrate:
- Cholesterol:

160. Halloween Punch

Serving: 24 servings. | Prep: 10mins | Cook: 0mins | Ready in:

Ingredients

- 1 can (46 ounces) pineapple juice, divided
- 1 package (3 ounces) orange gelatin
- 1 carton (64 ounces) orange juice
- 1 liter ginger ale, chilled
- 1 quart orange sherbet

Direction

- Boil 1 cup of pineapple juice in a saucepan. Mix in gelatin until dissolved completely. Cool; move to a container or large pitcher. Pour in orange juice and the rest of pineapple juice. Let chill. Pour into a punch bowl before serving; put in ginger ale and stir well. Add scoops of sherbet on top.

Nutrition Information

- Calories: 132 calories
- Protein: 1g protein.
- Total Fat: 1g fat (0 saturated fat)
- Sodium: 23mg sodium
- Fiber: 0 fiber)
- Total Carbohydrate: 31g carbohydrate (28g sugars
- Cholesterol: 1mg cholesterol

161. Herb Garden Tea

Serving: 9 servings. | Prep: 10mins | Cook: 0mins | Ready in:

Ingredients

- 1/4 cup finely chopped lemon balm
- 1/4 cup finely chopped fresh mint
- 1/4 cup lemon juice
- 1/4 cup orange juice
- 1/4 cup honey
- 2 liters ginger ale

Direction

- Combine the initial 5 ingredients in a small bowl and allow to stand for 1 hour. Strain then remove the herbs.
- Transfer the tea into a 2 – 1/2-quart pitcher. Right before serving, add in ginger ale and stir. Pour into chilled glasses to serve.

Nutrition Information

- Calories: 112 calories
- Fiber: 0 fiber)
- Total Carbohydrate: 29g carbohydrate (28g sugars
- Cholesterol: 0 cholesterol
- Protein: 0 protein.
- Total Fat: 0 fat (0 saturated fat)
- Sodium: 17mg sodium

162. Hibiscus Iced Tea

Serving: 1 serving. | Prep: 10mins | Cook: 0mins | Ready in:

Ingredients

- 1 cup water
- 5 dried hibiscus flowers or 1 teaspoon crushed dried hibiscus flowers
- Ice cubes

Direction

- Boil water in a saucepan. Take away from the heat. Place in hibiscus flowers and allow to stand for 5 minutes. Strain the tea in chilled glass over ice. Serve.

Nutrition Information

- Calories:
- Sodium:
- Fiber:
- Total Carbohydrate:
- Cholesterol:
- Protein:
- Total Fat:

163. Highbush Cranberry Tea

Serving: 3-1/4 quarts. | Prep: 5mins | Cook: 20mins | Ready in:

Ingredients

- 4 cups highbush cranberries
- 10 cups water, divided
- 2 to 3 cups sugar
- 1 cup red-hot candies
- 15 whole cloves
- 1 cup thawed orange juice concentrate
- 1/2 cup lemon juice

Direction

- Bring 4 cups water and cranberries in a big saucepan to a boil. Lower heat and simmer until berries pop, about 4 minutes. Press through a strainer and get rid of seeds and skins. Juice should measure approximately 4 1/2 cup, set aside.

- In a separate saucepan, mix together leftover water, cloves, candies and sugar, then bring the mixture to a boil. Lower heat and simmer until candies are dissolved, about 5 minutes. Strain and get rid of cloves. Whisk in the reserved cranberry juice, lemon juice and orange juice concentrate. Serve cold or hot.

Nutrition Information

- Calories:
- Total Fat:
- Sodium:
- Fiber:
- Total Carbohydrate:
- Cholesterol:
- Protein:

164. Holiday Mimosa

Serving: 6 | Prep: 10mins | Cook: | Ready in:

Ingredients

- 1/4 cup orange liqueur (such as Grand Marnier®)
- 2 tablespoons white sugar
- 1 cup orange juice
- 1 (750 milliliter) bottle brut champagne, chilled

Direction

- In a shallow bowl, pour out the orange liqueur and put the sugar in a saucer. In the orange liqueur, dip the rims of 6 glasses, adding sugar in order to form a sugared rim.
- Divide the remaining orange liqueur and orange juice among the 6 prepared glasses, pour champagne on top of the mixture and serve immediately.

165. Homemade Holiday Eggnog

Serving: 2 quarts. | Prep: 10mins | Cook: 25mins | Ready in:

Ingredients

- 8 eggs
- 1 cup sugar
- 3 cups milk, divided
- 3 cups heavy whipping cream, divided
- 1 teaspoon ground nutmeg

Direction

- Mix sugar, 1 cup cream, 1 cup milk and the eggs in a large heavy saucepan. Cook and stir on medium heat until a thermometer reads 160deg, about 25 minutes; or until mixture coats a metal spoon
- Dump into a large bowl; add in the remaining milk and cream, and nutmeg. Take an ice-water bath to place the bowl; stir constantly until cooled. Cover and store in refrigerator in minimum of 3 hours before serving.

Nutrition Information

- Calories:
- Total Fat:
- Sodium:
- Fiber:
- Total Carbohydrate:
- Cholesterol:
- Protein:

166. Homemade Lemonade

Serving: 6 servings, 1-1/3 cups each | Prep: 5mins | Cook: | Ready in:

Ingredients

- COUNTRY TIME Lemonade Flavor Drink Mix

- 2 qt. (8 cups) cold water
- Juice from 1 lemon
- 30 small mint leaves
- 1 lemon, cut into 6 slices

Direction

- 1. Measure into cap with 2-qt line drink mix then empty into 2-qt glass or plastic pitcher.
- 2. Put in lemon juice and water. Stir until the mixture has dissolved. In try sections with 30 ice cubes, add 2 1/2 cups lemonade. Add mint sprig to each section.
- 3. Place in the freezer for 3 hours until firm. Chill the leftover lemonade.
- 4. Divide into 6 tall glasses with frozen lemonade cubes then pour in prepared drink to fill. Decorate with lemon slices.

Nutrition Information

- Calories: 90
- Saturated Fat: 0 g
- Total Carbohydrate: 24 g
- Cholesterol: 0 mg
- Total Fat: 0 g
- Sodium: 40 mg
- Fiber: 1 g
- Sugar: 21 g
- Protein: 0 g

167. Homemade Limoncello

Serving: 1-1/2 quarts. | Prep: 30mins | Cook: 10mins | Ready in:

Ingredients

- 10 medium lemons
- 1 bottle (750 milliliters) vodka
- 3 cups water
- 1-1/2 cups sugar

Direction

- Peel rind from the lemons with a vegetable peeler. Reserve lemons for other uses. Use a sharp knife to scrape pith form the peels and remove. In a plastic container or a large glass, add vodka and lemon peels. Cover then allow to stand for at least 2 weeks at room temperature, stir once per week.
- Boil sugar and water in a large saucepan. Lower heat and simmer for 10 minutes, uncovered. Let cool completely.
- Strain the vodka mixture then remove lemon peels. Bring the mixture back to the container and stir in the sugar mixture. Transfer into glass bottles and seal tightly. Allow to stand for 2 weeks. Serve while chilled.

Nutrition Information

- Calories: 87 calories
- Protein: 0 protein.
- Total Fat: 0 fat (0 saturated fat)
- Sodium: 0 sodium
- Fiber: 0 fiber)
- Total Carbohydrate: 9g carbohydrate (9g sugars
- Cholesterol: 0 cholesterol

168. Honey Berry Milk Shakes

Serving: 4 servings. | Prep: 10mins | Cook: 0mins | Ready in:

Ingredients

- 1 pint vanilla ice cream or frozen yogurt
- 2-1/2 cups sliced fresh strawberries
- 1/2 cup milk
- 1/4 cup honey

Direction

- Mix honey, berries, ice cream, and milk in a blender. Cover it and process until smooth. Pour the processed drink into the glasses.

Nutrition Information

- Calories: 202 calories
- Total Fat: 1g fat (0 saturated fat)
- Sodium: 82mg sodium
- Fiber: 0 fiber)
- Total Carbohydrate: 45g carbohydrate (0 sugars
- Cholesterol: 2mg cholesterol
- Protein: 7g protein. Diabetic Exchanges: 1-1/2 starch

169. Honeydew Kiwi Cooler

Serving: 4 servings. | Prep: 5mins | Cook: 0mins | Ready in:

Ingredients

- 3 cups cubed honeydew melon
- 2 kiwifruit, peeled and cubed
- 1/2 cup fat-free plain yogurt
- 2 tablespoons honey
- 1 cup ice cubes
- 2 to 3 drops green food coloring, optional

Direction

- Mix all ingredients in a blender, then cover and blend until combined. Transfer into cold glasses and serve promptly.

Nutrition Information

- Calories: 113 calories
- Total Fat: 0 fat (0 saturated fat)
- Sodium: 32mg sodium
- Fiber: 2g fiber)
- Total Carbohydrate: 28g carbohydrate (0 sugars
- Cholesterol: 1mg cholesterol
- Protein: 2g protein. Diabetic Exchanges: 2 fruit.

170. Honeydew Lime Cooler

Serving: 5 servings. | Prep: 30mins | Cook: 0mins | Ready in:

Ingredients

- 4-1/2 cups cubed honeydew (about 1 small melon)
- 1-1/2 cups lime sherbet
- 2 tablespoons lime juice
- 5 fresh strawberries

Direction

- In a 15x10x1-inches baking pan, place the melon cubes and cover them. Allow them to freeze for about 15 minutes until firm. Reserve 5 melon cubes and set aside.
- Mix lime juice, remaining frozen melon, and sherbet in a food processor. Cover the food processor and process the mixture until smooth. Pour the mixture into the glasses. Garnish the glass with the reserved melon and strawberries.

Nutrition Information

- Calories: 135 calories
- Protein: 1g protein. Diabetic Exchanges: 1 starch
- Total Fat: 1g fat (0 saturated fat)
- Sodium: 34mg sodium
- Fiber: 1g fiber)
- Total Carbohydrate: 32g carbohydrate (28g sugars
- Cholesterol: 3mg cholesterol

171. Hop, Skip And Go

Serving: 4 servings. | Prep: 10mins | Cook: 0mins | Ready in:

Ingredients

- 3/4 cup thawed pink lemonade concentrate
- 1 bottle (12 ounces) beer
- 3 ounces vodka or rum
- 1 cup ice cubes
- GARNISH:
- Maraschino cherries

Direction

- Combine all of the ingredients in a blender. Cover and blend till smooth and the mixture will be foamy. Transfer into cocktail glasses and hurricane. Garnish as preferred.

Nutrition Information

- Calories: 184 calories
- Fiber: 0 fiber)
- Total Carbohydrate: 28g carbohydrate (25g sugars
- Cholesterol: 0 cholesterol
- Protein: 1g protein.
- Total Fat: 0 fat (0 saturated fat)
- Sodium: 6mg sodium

172. Horchata

Serving: 8 | Prep: 15mins | Cook: | Ready in:

Ingredients

- 2 quarts hot water
- 1/2 cup white sugar
- 1 1/2 teaspoons ground cinnamon
- 1 cup long grain rice
- 1 cup milk
- ice cubes, for serving

Direction

- Add rice, cinnamon and sugar in hot water and stir to dissolve the sugar. Cover and allow to stand for at least 3 hours or preferably overnight at room temperature.
- Add in milk, stir then use a hand blender to puree or puree in batches using a standing blender till the rice looks like fine sand. Strain through a very fine strainer or through several cheesecloth layers. Pour over ice to serve.

Nutrition Information

- Calories: 149 calories;
- Sodium: 25
- Total Carbohydrate: 32.8
- Cholesterol: 2
- Protein: 2.7
- Total Fat: 0.8

173. I'm A Little Teapot Tea

Serving: about 2 quarts. | Prep: 15mins | Cook: 0mins | Ready in:

Ingredients

- 4 cups cold water
- 1/2 cup sugar
- 1/2 cup sweetened lemonade drink mix
- 1 envelope unsweetened strawberry Kool-Aid mix
- 1 tablespoon lime juice
- 1 liter club soda, chilled

Direction

- Mix the first 5 ingredients in a big pitcher until dissolved. Stir in soda right before serving.

Nutrition Information

- Calories: 100 calories
- Total Fat: 0 fat (0 saturated fat)
- Sodium: 54mg sodium
- Fiber: 0 fiber)

- Total Carbohydrate: 26g carbohydrate (19g sugars
- Cholesterol: 0 cholesterol
- Protein: 0 protein.

174. Iced Coffee Latte

Serving: Makes 5 servings, 1 cup each. | Prep: 10mins | Cook: | Ready in:

Ingredients

- 6 Tbsp. ground MAXWELL HOUSE Coffee, any variety
- 3 cups cold water
- 2 cups milk

Direction

- Add coffee in filter in coffee maker's brew basket. Pour water in coffee maker then brew. Let it completely cool.
- Add coffee into pitcher. Stir in milk till well blended. Store in the fridge till ready to serve or serve immediately.
- Pour over ice cubes in 5 tall glasses to serve.

Nutrition Information

- Calories: 60
- Saturated Fat: 1 g
- Sodium: 50 mg
- Fiber: 1 g
- Total Fat: 2 g
- Sugar: 5 g
- Total Carbohydrate: 7 g
- Cholesterol: 10 mg
- Protein: 4 g

175. Iced Coffee Slush

Serving: 12 servings (2-1/4 quarts). | Prep: 10mins | Cook: 0mins | Ready in:

Ingredients

- 3 cups hot strong brewed coffee
- 1-1/2 to 2 cups sugar
- 4 cups milk
- 2 cups half-and-half cream
- 1-1/2 teaspoons vanilla extract

Direction

- Stir sugar and coffee in a freezer-safe bowl till sugar dissolves. Store in the fridge till thoroughly chilled. Add vanilla, cream and milk; freeze. Several hours before serving, take away from the freezer. Chop mixture till slushy then immediately serve.

Nutrition Information

- Calories: 202 calories
- Sodium: 61mg sodium
- Fiber: 0 fiber)
- Total Carbohydrate: 30g carbohydrate (29g sugars
- Cholesterol: 31mg cholesterol
- Protein: 4g protein.
- Total Fat: 7g fat (4g saturated fat)

176. Iced Honeydew Mint Tea

Serving: 10 servings. | Prep: 15mins | Cook: 5mins | Ready in:

Ingredients

- 4 cups water
- 24 fresh mint leaves
- 8 individual green tea bags
- 2/3 cup sugar
- 5 cups diced honeydew melon, divided

- 3 cups ice cubes, divided
- Additional ice cubes

Direction

- Bring water in a big saucepan to a boil then take away from heat. Put in tea bags and mint leaves, allow to soak for 3-5 minutes depending on taste, with a cover, while stirring sometimes. Get rid of the tea bags and mint. Whisk sugar in.
- In a blender, add 1 1/2 cups ice, 2 cups tea and 2 1/2 cups honey dew, then cover and blend until combined. Serve over with more ice. Do the same process for the leftover ingredients.

Nutrition Information

- Calories: 83 calories
- Fiber: 1g fiber)
- Total Carbohydrate: 21g carbohydrate (20g sugars
- Cholesterol: 0 cholesterol
- Protein: 0 protein. Diabetic Exchanges: 1 starch
- Total Fat: 0 fat (0 saturated fat)
- Sodium: 15mg sodium

177. Iced Lemon Tea

Serving: 12 servings (1 cup each). | Prep: 10mins | Cook: 10mins | Ready in:

Ingredients

- 3-1/2 teaspoons Crystal Light lemonade drink mix
- 4 cups cold water
- 8 cups water
- 8 individual decaffeinated tea bags
- 1 mint-flavored black tea bag
- Ice cubes
- Fresh mint leaves and lemon slices, optional

Direction

- Combine cold water and lemonade mix in a large pitcher. Store in the fridge to chill.
- In the meantime, boil water in a large saucepan. Take away from the heat and place in tea bags. Let steep for 3-5 minutes, covered. Remove the tea bags. Let cool and add in lemonade mixture, stir. Pour over ice to serve, add lemon and mint if preferred.

Nutrition Information

- Calories: 3 calories
- Sodium: 1mg sodium
- Fiber: 0 fiber)
- Total Carbohydrate: 0 carbohydrate (0 sugars
- Cholesterol: 0 cholesterol
- Protein: 0 protein.
- Total Fat: 0 fat (0 saturated fat)

178. Iced Melon Moroccan Mint Tea

Serving: 5 servings. | Prep: 20mins | Cook: 0mins | Ready in:

Ingredients

- 2 cups water
- 12 fresh mint leaves
- 4 individual green tea bags
- 1/3 cup sugar
- 2-1/2 cups diced honeydew melon
- 1-1/2 cups ice cubes
- Additional ice cubes

Direction

- Bring water in a big saucepan to a boil. Take away from heat then put in tea bags and mint. Cover and allow to soak for 3 to 5 minutes. Get rid of tea bags and mint then whisk in sugar.
- Blend honeydew in a blender, until combined. Put in tea and 1 1/2 cups ice, process until blended. Serve over more ice.

Nutrition Information

- Calories: 81 calories
- Protein: 0 protein. Diabetic Exchanges: 1 starch.
- Total Fat: 0 fat (0 saturated fat)
- Sodium: 9mg sodium
- Fiber: 1g fiber)
- Total Carbohydrate: 21g carbohydrate (21g sugars
- Cholesterol: 0 cholesterol

179. Iced Strawberry Tea

Serving: 5 cups. | Prep: 10mins | Cook: 0mins | Ready in:

Ingredients

- 1 pint fresh strawberries
- 4 cups brewed tea, chilled
- 1/3 to 1/2 cup sugar
- 1/4 cup lemon juice
- Ice cubes

Direction

- Put aside 5 strawberries. Into a blender, add the leftover strawberries then cover and puree. Strain the mixture into a pitcher. Add lemon juice, sugar and tea then stir to dissolve the sugar. Chill.
- Pour over ice in chilled glasses to serve. Add reserved berries for garnish.

Nutrition Information

- Calories: 74 calories
- Cholesterol: 0 cholesterol
- Protein: 0 protein.
- Total Fat: 0 fat (0 saturated fat)
- Sodium: 7mg sodium
- Fiber: 1g fiber)

- Total Carbohydrate: 19g carbohydrate (16g sugars

180. Icy Holiday Punch

Serving: 30 servings (about 5-3/4 quarts). | Prep: 10mins | Cook: 0mins | Ready in:

Ingredients

- 1 package (6 ounces) cherry gelatin
- 3/4 cup sugar
- 2 cups boiling water
- 1 can (46 ounces) unsweetened pineapple juice
- 6 cups cold water
- 2 liters ginger ale, chilled

Direction

- Dissolve sugar and gelatin in boiling water in a 4-quart freezer-proof container. Mix in cold water and pineapple juice. Leave in the freezer with a cover overnight. Take out of the freezer 2 hours prior to serving. Arrange into a punch bowl; mix in ginger ale just prior to serving.

Nutrition Information

- Calories: 89 calories
- Total Carbohydrate: 22g carbohydrate (21g sugars
- Cholesterol: 0 cholesterol
- Protein: 1g protein.
- Total Fat: 0 fat (0 saturated fat)
- Sodium: 19mg sodium
- Fiber: 0 fiber)

181. Icy Lemonade

Serving: 10 cups. | Prep: 5mins | Cook: 0mins | Ready in:

Ingredients

- 1 can (12 ounces) frozen lemonade concentrate
- 30 to 35 ice cubes
- 4 cups lemon-lime soda, chilled

Direction

- In a blender, add 15 to 17 ice cubes and 1/2 of the lemonade concentrate. Put in 2 cups soda. Cover and blend on high until ice is crushed. Repeat. Serve promptly in cold glass.

Nutrition Information

- Calories: 101 calories
- Cholesterol: 0 cholesterol
- Protein: 0 protein.
- Total Fat: 0 fat (0 saturated fat)
- Sodium: 12mg sodium
- Fiber: 0 fiber)
- Total Carbohydrate: 26g carbohydrate (24g sugars

182. Irish Creme Drink

Serving: 10 servings (1/2 cup each). | Prep: 10mins | Cook: 0mins | Ready in:

Ingredients

- 3-1/2 cups vanilla ice cream, softened
- 3/4 cup vodka
- 1/2 cup eggnog
- 1/3 cup sweetened condensed milk
- 1 tablespoon chocolate syrup
- 1 teaspoon instant coffee granules
- 1/2 teaspoon vanilla extract
- 1/4 teaspoon almond extract
- Grated chocolate and additional chocolate syrup

Direction

- Combine the initial 8 ingredients in a large bowl and beat till smooth. Put aside.
- In separate shallow bowls, place additional chocolate syrup and grated chocolate. Hold each glass upside down then dip its rim in chocolate syrup then grated chocolate. Transfer the drink mixture into the prepped glasses. Serve at once.

Nutrition Information

- Calories: 218 calories
- Cholesterol: 35mg cholesterol
- Protein: 4g protein.
- Total Fat: 8g fat (5g saturated fat)
- Sodium: 70mg sodium
- Fiber: 0 fiber)
- Total Carbohydrate: 25g carbohydrate (21g sugars

183. Irish Whiskey Float

Serving: 1 serving. | Prep: 5mins | Cook: 0mins | Ready in:

Ingredients

- 1 scoop vanilla ice cream
- 1 cup cola
- 1 ounce Irish whiskey

Direction

- In a tall glass, place ice cream then pour whiskey and cola over the top. Serve at once.

Nutrition Information

- Calories: 299 calories
- Total Fat: 7g fat (4g saturated fat)
- Sodium: 63mg sodium
- Fiber: 0 fiber)
- Total Carbohydrate: 41g carbohydrate (37g sugars
- Cholesterol: 29mg cholesterol
- Protein: 2g protein.

184. Kiwi Smoothies

Serving: 4 servings. | Prep: 10mins | Cook: 0mins | Ready in:

Ingredients

- 3 kiwifruit, peeled and cut into chunks
- 2 medium ripe bananas, cut into 4 pieces and frozen
- 1 cup frozen blueberries
- 1 cup (8 ounces) fat-free plain yogurt
- 3 tablespoons honey
- 1/4 teaspoon almond extract, optional
- 1-1/2 cups crushed ice

Direction

- Mix together honey, fruit, yogurt and extract, if you want, in a blender. Cover and blend until blended. Put in ice, then cover and process until combined, whisking if needed. Transfer into cold glasses and serve promptly.

Nutrition Information

- Calories: 196 calories
- Protein: 5g protein.
- Total Fat: 1g fat (0 saturated fat)
- Sodium: 48mg sodium
- Fiber: 5g fiber)
- Total Carbohydrate: 46g carbohydrate (37g sugars
- Cholesterol: 1mg cholesterol

185. Lean Green Smoothie

Serving: 4 | Prep: 10mins | Cook: | Ready in:

Ingredients

- 3 cups honeydew melon - peeled, seeded and cubed
- 3 cups ice cubes
- 1 cup green grapes
- 1 cucumber, peeled and chopped
- 1/2 cup broccoli florets (optional)
- 1 sprig fresh mint

Direction

- Puree ice cubes, broccoli, mint, grapes, honeydew melon, and cucumber in a blender until smooth. Cover.

Nutrition Information

- Calories: 86 calories;
- Cholesterol: 0
- Protein: 1.6
- Total Fat: 0.5
- Sodium: 35
- Total Carbohydrate: 21.2

186. Lemon Berry Pitcher Punch

Serving: about 3 cups. | Prep: 5mins | Cook: 0mins | Ready in:

Ingredients

- 1/4 cup sweetened lemonade drink mix
- 2 cups cold water
- 1/3 cup cranberry juice, chilled
- 3/4 cup lemon-lime soda, chilled

Direction

- Mix cranberry juice, water and drink mix in a pitcher. Stir in soda and serve promptly.

Nutrition Information

- Calories: 9 calories

- Sodium: 3mg sodium
- Fiber: 0 fiber)
- Total Carbohydrate: 1g carbohydrate (0 sugars
- Cholesterol: 0 cholesterol
- Protein: 0 protein.
- Total Fat: 0 fat (0 saturated fat)

187. Lemon Pineapple Smoothies

Serving: 4 servings. | Prep: 5mins | Cook: 0mins | Ready in:

Ingredients

- 2 cups vanilla ice cream
- 1 can (20 ounces) pineapple tidbits, drained
- 1 cup chilled lemon-lime soda
- 2 tablespoons lemonade concentrate
- 1 drop yellow food coloring, optional

Direction

- Mix all ingredients in a blender then cover and blend until smooth. Transfer into cold glasses and serve promptly.

Nutrition Information

- Calories: 225 calories
- Sodium: 66mg sodium
- Fiber: 1g fiber)
- Total Carbohydrate: 40g carbohydrate (34g sugars
- Cholesterol: 29mg cholesterol
- Protein: 3g protein.
- Total Fat: 7g fat (4g saturated fat)

188. Lemon Refresher

Serving: 3 quarts. | Prep: 15mins | Cook: 0mins | Ready in:

Ingredients

- 1-1/2 cups sugar
- 1/3 cup lemon juice
- 2 cups whole milk
- 1 tablespoon lemon extract
- 1/2 teaspoon grated lemon zest, optional
- 2 liters lemon-lime soda, chilled
- Ice cubes

Direction

- Beat lemon juice and sugar for 3 minutes on high speed in a big bowl, until sugar is almost dissolved. Gently beat in milk. Stir in lemon extract and lemon zest if you want. Refrigerate. Right before serving, stir in soda and serve over ice in cold glass.

Nutrition Information

- Calories: 198 calories
- Fiber: 0 fiber)
- Total Carbohydrate: 45g carbohydrate (44g sugars
- Cholesterol: 6mg cholesterol
- Protein: 1g protein.
- Total Fat: 1g fat (1g saturated fat)
- Sodium: 39mg sodium

189. Lemon Orange Iced Tea

Serving: 10 servings. | Prep: 20mins | Cook: 0mins | Ready in:

Ingredients

- 2 quarts cold water, divided
- 6 individual tea bags
- 2 sprigs fresh mint
- 3-1/2 teaspoons Crystal Light lemonade drink mix
- 2 cups orange juice

Direction

- Boil 1 quart of water in a saucepan. Take away from the heat. Place in mint and tea bags then allow to stand for 10 minutes.
- Remove mint and tea bags. Transfer the tea into a large pitcher. Pour in the leftover water, orange juice and lemonade drink mix then stir well. Store in the fridge to chill. Pour over ice to serve.

Nutrition Information

- Calories: 27 calories
- Protein: 0 protein. Diabetic Exchanges: 1/2 fruit.
- Total Fat: 0 fat (0 saturated fat)
- Sodium: 1mg sodium
- Fiber: 0 fiber)
- Total Carbohydrate: 5g carbohydrate (0 sugars
- Cholesterol: 0 cholesterol

190. Leprechaun Lime Punch

Serving: 20-24 servings (1 gallon). | Prep: 10mins | Cook: 0mins | Ready in:

Ingredients

- 5-3/4 cups refrigerated citrus punch
- 2 cans (12 ounces each) frozen limeade concentrate, thawed
- 1/4 cup sugar
- 1/4 cup lime juice
- 1 quart lime sherbet, softened
- 2 liters lemon-lime soda, chilled
- 5 drops green food coloring
- Lime slices

Direction

- Mix together sherbet, lime juice, sugar, limeade and citrus punch on a big punch bowl or pitcher, then stir mixture until smooth and sugar has dissolved. Put in food coloring and soda, stirring to combine. Float on top with slices of lime, then serve instantly.

Nutrition Information

- Calories: 128 calories
- Total Fat: 1g fat (0 saturated fat)
- Sodium: 25mg sodium
- Fiber: 0 fiber)
- Total Carbohydrate: 32g carbohydrate (29g sugars
- Cholesterol: 1mg cholesterol
- Protein: 0 protein.

191. Lime Fizz

Serving: 1 serving. | Prep: 5mins | Cook: 0mins | Ready in:

Ingredients

- 1/2 to 3/4 cup ice cubes
- 3 lime wedges
- 1 cup club soda, chilled
- Sugar substitute equivalent to 1 teaspoon sugar

Direction

- In a highball glass, place ice and squeeze over with lime wedges; let the limes drop into the glass. Gradually add in club soda then add sugar substitute in the glass and stir. Serve at once.

Nutrition Information

- Calories: 6 calories
- Cholesterol: 0 cholesterol
- Protein: 0 protein.
- Total Fat: 0 fat (0 saturated fat)
- Sodium: 51mg sodium
- Fiber: 0 fiber)

- Total Carbohydrate: 2g carbohydrate (1g sugars

192. Lime Milk Shakes

Serving: 6 servings. | Prep: 10mins | Cook: 0mins | Ready in:

Ingredients

- 2-1/4 cups milk
- 3/4 cup thawed limeade concentrate
- 3 cups lime sherbet, softened

Direction

- In a blender, combine all the ingredients and process them, covered, until smooth. Pour the drink into the chilled glasses to serve.

Nutrition Information

- Calories: 251 calories
- Sodium: 71mg sodium
- Fiber: 2g fiber)
- Total Carbohydrate: 49g carbohydrate (44g sugars
- Cholesterol: 9mg cholesterol
- Protein: 4g protein.
- Total Fat: 4g fat (3g saturated fat)

193. Lime Milk Shakes For Two

Serving: 2 servings. | Prep: 5mins | Cook: 0mins | Ready in:

Ingredients

- 3/4 cup milk
- 1/4 cup thawed limeade concentrate
- 1 cup sherbet, softened

Direction

- Combine all the ingredients in a blender. Cover the blender and process the mixture until smooth. Pour the mixture into the chilled glasses. Serve.

Nutrition Information

- Calories: 251 calories
- Protein: 4g protein.
- Total Fat: 4g fat (3g saturated fat)
- Sodium: 71mg sodium
- Fiber: 2g fiber)
- Total Carbohydrate: 49g carbohydrate (44g sugars
- Cholesterol: 9mg cholesterol

194. Lime Paradise

Serving: 2 servings. | Prep: 10mins | Cook: 0mins | Ready in:

Ingredients

- 1/4 cup fresh mint leaves
- 1/4 cup lime juice
- 2 tablespoons sugar
- Ice cubes
- 2 cups water

Direction

- Muddle sugar, lime juice and mint in 2 rocks glasses. Place in ice then add in water.

Nutrition Information

- Calories: 62 calories
- Fiber: 1g fiber)
- Total Carbohydrate: 16g carbohydrate (14g sugars
- Cholesterol: 0 cholesterol

- Protein: 1g protein. Diabetic Exchanges: 1 starch.
- Total Fat: 0 fat (0 saturated fat)
- Sodium: 4mg sodium

195. Lime Sherbet Slush

Serving: 5 servings. | Prep: 5mins | Cook: 0mins | Ready in:

Ingredients

- 1 pint lime sherbet
- 1-1/2 cups diet lemon-lime soda, chilled
- 3/4 cup limade concentrate
- 1 teaspoon grated lime zest
- 14 ice cubes

Direction

- Mix all ingredients in a food processor or a blender. Cover and blend until smooth. Transfer into glasses and serve promptly.

Nutrition Information

- Calories: 173 calories
- Cholesterol: 5mg cholesterol
- Protein: 1g protein. Diabetic Exchanges: 3 fruit.
- Total Fat: 2g fat (1g saturated fat)
- Sodium: 43mg sodium
- Fiber: 1g fiber
- Total Carbohydrate: 41g carbohydrate (0 sugars

196. Limoncello Spritzer

Serving: 1 | Prep: 5mins | Cook: | Ready in:

Ingredients

- 1 cup ice cubes, or as needed
- 2 lemon slices, divided
- 2 tablespoons frozen lemonade concentrate
- 2 tablespoons limoncello liqueur
- 4 fluid ounces club soda, or as needed

Direction

- Add ice cubes to fill a tall glass. In the glass, place 1 lemon slice then add lemonade concentrate and pour in limocello. Fill glass with enough club soda and stir well. Garnish with another lemon slice on the rim of the glass.

Nutrition Information

- Calories: 109 calories;
- Cholesterol: 0
- Protein: 0.4
- Total Fat: 0.2
- Sodium: 14
- Total Carbohydrate: 24.7

197. Long Island Iced Tea

Serving: 1 | Prep: 5mins | Cook: | Ready in:

Ingredients

- 1 (1.5 fluid ounce) jigger vodka
- 1 (1.5 fluid ounce) jigger gin
- 1 (1.5 fluid ounce) jigger rum
- 1 (1.5 fluid ounce) jigger triple sec liqueur
- 1 teaspoon tequila
- 2 teaspoons orange juice
- 2 fluid ounces cola-flavored carbonated beverage
- 1 wedge lemon

Direction

- Fill the cocktail mixer with full ice and stir in gin, triple sec, tequila, rum, and vodka. Mix in cola and orange juice. Shake the mixer vigorously until foamy. Transfer the mixture into the Collins glass and fill it with ice. Garnish the glass with lemon wedge before serving.

Nutrition Information

- Calories: 507 calories;
- Total Fat: 0.2
- Sodium: 8
- Total Carbohydrate: 28.9
- Cholesterol: 0
- Protein: 0.3

198. Lost In The Sun Punch

Serving: 16-20 servings (4 quarts). | Prep: 5mins | Cook: 0mins | Ready in:

Ingredients

- 1 carton (64 ounces) orange juice, chilled
- 1 bottle (2 liters) lemonade, chilled
- 6 cans (12 ounces each) cream soda, chilled
- 1 pint pineapple sherbet

Direction

- Combine cream soda, lemonade and orange juice in a large punch bowl. Place scoops of sherbet on top. Serve at once.

Nutrition Information

- Calories: 115 calories
- Protein: 1g protein.
- Total Fat: 0 fat (0 saturated fat)
- Sodium: 15mg sodium
- Fiber: 0 fiber)
- Total Carbohydrate: 28g carbohydrate (24g sugars
- Cholesterol: 1mg cholesterol

199. Luscious Lime Slush

Serving: 28 servings (3/4 cup each). | Prep: 10mins | Cook: 10mins | Ready in:

Ingredients

- 9 cups water
- 4 individual green tea bags
- 2 cans (12 ounces each) frozen limeade concentrate, thawed
- 2 cups sugar
- 2 cups lemon rum or rum
- 7 cups lemon-lime soda, chilled

Direction

- Bring water to a boil in a Dutch oven. Take away from heat then put in tea bags. Cover and soak about 3 to 5 minutes, then get rid of tea bags. Stir in rum, sugar and limeade concentrate.
- Turn to a 4-qt. freezer container and let it cool. Cover and place in the freezer about 6 hours or overnight.
- To serve frozen limeade mixture: In a 4-qt. pitcher, mix soda and the limeade mixture together. For each serving, mix in a glass with 1/4 cup soda and 1/2 cup limeade mixture then serve promptly.

Nutrition Information

- Calories: 177 calories
- Protein: 0 protein.
- Total Fat: 0 fat (0 saturated fat)
- Sodium: 7mg sodium
- Fiber: 0 fiber)
- Total Carbohydrate: 36g carbohydrate (35g sugars
- Cholesterol: 0 cholesterol

200. Mad Scientist Punch

Serving: 16 servings (4 quarts). | Prep: 15mins | Cook: 0mins | Ready in:

Ingredients

- 2 cans (12 ounces each) frozen pineapple-orange juice concentrate, thawed
- 2 cups water
- 1 envelope unsweetened orange Kool-Aid mix
- 2 liters lemon-lime soda, chilled
- 1 pint orange sherbet, softened

Direction

- Mix the Kool-Aid mix, water and juice concentrate in a punch bowl. Mix in soda. Add scoops of sherbet on top. Serve right away.

Nutrition Information

- Calories: 159 calories
- Sodium: 51mg sodium
- Fiber: 0 fiber)
- Total Carbohydrate: 38g carbohydrate (35g sugars
- Cholesterol: 1mg cholesterol
- Protein: 1g protein.
- Total Fat: 0 fat (0 saturated fat)

201. Make Ahead Rhubarb Slush

Serving: 12 servings. | Prep: 20mins | Cook: 0mins | Ready in:

Ingredients

- 8 cups sliced fresh or frozen rhubarb
- 8 cups water
- 3 cups sugar
- 1/2 cup lemon juice
- 1 package (3 ounces) strawberry gelatin
- Lemon-lime soda, optional

Direction

- Mix together lemon juice, sugar, water and rhubarb in a big kettle then cook until the rhubarb is softened. Strain and save juice. Put gelatin in the hot juice and stir until gelatin is dissolved. Transfer into individual plastic cups or a 5-qt. container, then place in the freezer.
- Let the mixture thaw until slushy to serve. Put in 2 tbsp. lemon-lime soda to each serving if wanted.

Nutrition Information

- Calories: 239 calories
- Protein: 1g protein.
- Total Fat: 0 fat (0 saturated fat)
- Sodium: 20mg sodium
- Fiber: 2g fiber)
- Total Carbohydrate: 61g carbohydrate (57g sugars
- Cholesterol: 0 cholesterol

202. Makeover Nutty Monkey Malts

Serving: 5 servings. | Prep: 5mins | Cook: 0mins | Ready in:

Ingredients

- 1/4 cup fat-free milk
- 1 small banana, cut into chunks
- 1/4 cup chocolate malted milk powder
- 2 tablespoons reduced-fat creamy peanut butter
- 2 cups fat-free frozen chocolate yogurt
- Whipped cream, optional

Direction

- In a blender, combine the malted milk powder, milk, peanut butter, and banana and process the mixture, covered, for 10 seconds until smooth. Add the frozen yogurt and cover

it again. Process for 10 more seconds or until well-blended. You can stir it if needed.
- Pour the drink into the chilled glasses. If desired, garnish the drink with whipped cream and serve immediately.

Nutrition Information

- Calories: 203 calories
- Total Fat: 3g fat (1g saturated fat)
- Sodium: 190mg sodium
- Fiber: 3g fiber)
- Total Carbohydrate: 39g carbohydrate (29g sugars
- Cholesterol: 1mg cholesterol
- Protein: 8g protein.

203. Mango Lassi

Serving: Makes 6 to 8 servings | Prep: | Cook: |Ready in:

Ingredients

- 3/4 cup peeled and chopped mango
- 3/4 cup low-fat yogurt
- 3 tablespoons sugar
- 1/4 cup milk
- 1/2 teaspoon lemon juice
- 1/4 cup mango sorbet
- 9 to 10 ice cubes

Direction

- In a blender, puree together sugar, yogurt and mango. Put in sorbet, lemon juice and milk then process until smooth. Put in ice and 1/3 cup of cold water and blend until get wanted consistency. Transfer into two small glasses or a tall glass. Serve together with a straw.

204. Mango Tango Smoothies

Serving: 2 servings. | Prep: 10mins | Cook: 0mins | Ready in:

Ingredients

- 1 cup chopped peeled mango
- 1 medium ripe banana, frozen, peeled and sliced
- 1 cup fat-free milk
- 1/2 cup reduced-fat plain yogurt
- 1/2 cup unsweetened pineapple juice

Direction

- Mix all ingredients in a blender then cover and blend until smooth. Transfer into cold glasses and serve promptly.

Nutrition Information

- Calories: 224 calories
- Total Fat: 2g fat (1g saturated fat)
- Sodium: 109mg sodium
- Fiber: 3g fiber)
- Total Carbohydrate: 47g carbohydrate (42g sugars
- Cholesterol: 6mg cholesterol
- Protein: 9g protein.

205. Mango Green Tea Smoothies

Serving: 2 cups. | Prep: 10mins | Cook: 0mins |Ready in:

Ingredients

- 1-1/2 cups frozen chopped peeled mangoes
- 1/2 cup brewed green tea, chilled
- 3 to 4 tablespoons lime juice
- 1 tablespoon honey
- 1 cup low-fat vanilla frozen yogurt

Direction

- Mix together honey, lime juice, tea and mangoes in a blender, then cover and blend until combined. Put in frozen yogurt, cover and process more until smooth. Transfer into cold glasses and serve promptly.

Nutrition Information

- Calories: 259 calories
- Fiber: 2g fiber)
- Total Carbohydrate: 53g carbohydrate (44g sugars
- Cholesterol: 15mg cholesterol
- Protein: 4g protein.
- Total Fat: 5g fat (3g saturated fat)
- Sodium: 50mg sodium

206. Martini

Serving: 1 | Prep: 2mins | Cook: | Ready in:

Ingredients

- 2 1/2 fluid ounces gin
- 1/2 fluid ounce dry vermouth
- 1 pitted green olive
- 1 cup ice

Direction

- Place ice into a shaker. Add in vermouth and gin. Cover and shake gently to mix gin and vermouth. Pour drink into a cocktail glass without ice. Gently drop into the glass lemon twist or olive. Serve.

207. Mint Tea Punch

Serving: 10 | Prep: 10mins | Cook: | Ready in:

Ingredients

- 3 cups boiling water
- 12 sprigs fresh mint
- 4 tea bags
- 1 cup white sugar
- 1 cup orange juice
- 1/4 cup lemon juice
- 5 cups cold water
- 3 orange slices for garnish (optional)
- 3 lemon slices for garnish (optional)

Direction

- In a large pitcher, place mint sprigs and tea bag then pour over with boiling water; let steep for 8 minutes. Remove and throw away mint leaves and tea bags, squeeze out the excess liquid. Add sugar and stir to dissolve; stir in lemon juice and orange juice. Add cold water. Pour over ice cubes and add lemon or orange slices for garnish. Serve.

Nutrition Information

- Calories: 94 calories;
- Protein: 0.4
- Total Fat: 0.1
- Sodium: 6
- Total Carbohydrate: 24.2
- Cholesterol: 0

208. Minted Raspberry Lemonade

Serving: 7 servings. | Prep: 20mins | Cook: 0mins | Ready in:

Ingredients

- 1/2 cup unsweetened raspberries
- 1 cup lemon juice (about 4 medium lemons)
- 3/4 cup sugar
- 1 teaspoon minced fresh mint or 1/4 teaspoon dried mint flakes
- 6 cups water

Direction

- Mash and strain raspberries, get rid of seeds and pulp while save juice. Mix mint, sugar and lemon juice in a punch bowl or a big container. Stir in saved raspberry juice and water. Serve in cold glass over ice.

Nutrition Information

- Calories: 88 calories
- Sodium: 1mg sodium
- Fiber: 0 fiber)
- Total Carbohydrate: 23g carbohydrate (0 sugars
- Cholesterol: 0 cholesterol
- Protein: 0 protein. Diabetic Exchanges: 1-1/2 fruit.
- Total Fat: 0 fat (0 saturated fat)

209. Minty Orange Lemonade

Serving: 3 quarts. | Prep: 15mins | Cook: 0mins | Ready in:

Ingredients

- 2-1/2 cups water
- 1-1/2 cups sugar
- 1-1/3 cups lemon juice
- 3/4 cup mint leaves
- 2/3 cup orange juice
- 4 teaspoons grated orange zest
- 7 cups cold water
- Orange slices and mint sprigs

Direction

- Mix sugar and water in a big saucepan then bring to a boil. Lower heat then cover and simmer about 5 minutes. Take away from heat then put in orange zest and juice, mint and lemon juice. Allow to stand for an hour.
- Strain and get rid of the orange zest and mint. Put in cold water and serve over ice. Decorate with orange slices and mint.

Nutrition Information

- Calories: 113 calories
- Sodium: 2mg sodium
- Fiber: 1g fiber)
- Total Carbohydrate: 29g carbohydrate (26g sugars
- Cholesterol: 0 cholesterol
- Protein: 0 protein.
- Total Fat: 0 fat (0 saturated fat)

210. Mixed Berry Sangria

Serving: 10 servings (3/4 cup each). | Prep: 10mins | Cook: 0mins | Ready in:

Ingredients

- 1 bottle (750 milliliters) sparkling white wine
- 2-1/2 cups white cranberry juice
- 2/3 cup light or coconut rum
- 1/3 cup each fresh blackberries, blueberries and raspberries
- 1/3 cup chopped fresh strawberries
- Ice cubes

Direction

- Mix rum, juice and wine in a large pitcher then place in fruit. Store in the fridge for at least 2 hours. Pour over ice to serve.

Nutrition Information

- Calories: 134 calories
- Sodium: 5mg sodium
- Fiber: 1g fiber)
- Total Carbohydrate: 12g carbohydrate (10g sugars
- Cholesterol: 0 cholesterol

- Protein: 0 protein.
- Total Fat: 0 fat (0 saturated fat)

211. Mocha Cappuccino Punch

Serving: 13 servings (3/4 cup each). | Prep: 15mins | Cook: 0mins | Ready in:

Ingredients

- 1 cup hot water
- 2 tablespoons instant coffee granules
- 1/4 teaspoon ground cinnamon
- 1 can (14 ounces) fat-free sweetened condensed milk
- 1/2 cup chocolate syrup
- 1 quart half-and-half cream
- 1 quart chocolate ice cream
- 2 cups club soda, chilled
- Baking cocoa

Direction

- Whisk cinnamon, coffee granules and water in a small bowl to dissolve the coffee granules. Add in chocolate syrup and milk; stir. Cover and store in the fridge to chill.
- Pour the milk mixture in a punch bowl; add in half-and-half cream and stir. Place in scoops of ice cream then slowly add in club soda. Use cocoa to dust the top. Serve at once.

Nutrition Information

- Calories: 305 calories
- Total Carbohydrate: 40g carbohydrate (38g sugars
- Cholesterol: 55mg cholesterol
- Protein: 7g protein.
- Total Fat: 12g fat (8g saturated fat)
- Sodium: 115mg sodium
- Fiber: 1g fiber)

212. Mocha Cooler

Serving: 14 | Prep: 15mins | Cook: | Ready in:

Ingredients

- 1/4 cup instant coffee granules
- 1 cup sugar
- 1 cup nonfat dry milk powder
- 1 cup powdered non-dairy creamer
- 1/3 cup baking cocoa
- 1/4 teaspoon salt
- ADDITIONAL INGREDIENTS:
- 1 1/2 cups crushed ice
- 1/2 cup milk
- whipped topping

Direction

- Crush coffee granules between sheets of waxed paper with a rolling pin till it becomes fine powder. Keep in an airtight container. Mix in salt, cocoa, creamer, milk powder and sugar. Place for up to 1 year in a cool dry place.
- For cooler preparing: Combine 1/2 cup of mocha mix, milk and ice in a blender. Cover and process till smooth on high. Transfer into glass. Place whipped topping on top if preferred.

213. Mock Champagne Punch

Serving: 16 (1/2-cup) servings. | Prep: 10mins | Cook: 0mins | Ready in:

Ingredients

- 1 quart white grape juice, chilled
- 1 quart ginger ale, chilled
- Strawberries or raspberries

Direction

- In glasses or a punch bowl, combine ginger ale and grape juice. Add berries for garnish.

Nutrition Information

- Calories: 58 calories
- Sodium: 8mg sodium
- Fiber: 0 fiber)
- Total Carbohydrate: 14g carbohydrate (14g sugars
- Cholesterol: 0 cholesterol
- Protein: 0 protein.
- Total Fat: 0 fat (0 saturated fat)

214. Mock Mint Julep

Serving: 13 servings (about 3 quarts). | Prep: 15mins | Cook: 0mins | Ready in:

Ingredients

- 2 cups cold water
- 1-1/2 cups sugar
- 3/4 cup lemon juice
- 6 mint sprigs
- 5 cups ice cubes
- 2-1/2 cups ginger ale, chilled
- Lemon slices and additional mint, optional

Direction

- Combine mint, lemon juice, sugar and water in a large bowl. Allow to stand for at least 45 minutes.
- Strain and remove mint. In two 2-quart pitchers, place ice cubes then pour ginger ale and 1/2 of the lemon mixture into each. Add mint and lemon for garnish if preferred.

Nutrition Information

- Calories:
- Sodium:
- Fiber:
- Total Carbohydrate:
- Cholesterol:
- Protein:
- Total Fat:

215. Mock Strawberry Margaritas

Serving: 6 servings. | Prep: 10mins | Cook: 0mins | Ready in:

Ingredients

- 6 lime wedges
- 3 tablespoons plus 1/3 cup sugar, divided
- 1-1/4 cups water
- 1 can (6 ounces) frozen limeade concentrate, partially thawed
- 1 package (16 ounces) frozen unsweetened strawberries
- 25 ice cubes

Direction

- Wet the rim of 6 glasses with lime wedges. Set limes aside for decorating. On a plate, spread 3 tbsp. sugar. Dip each glass's rim into sugar by holding upside down and set aside. Get rid of the leftover sugar on the plate.
- Mix together remaining sugar, ice cubes, limeade concentrate, strawberries and water in a blender. Cover and process until smooth. Transfer into prepared glasses and decorate with reserved limes. Serve promptly.

Nutrition Information

- Calories: 149 calories
- Protein: 0 protein.
- Total Fat: 0 fat (0 saturated fat)
- Sodium: 2mg sodium
- Fiber: 2g fiber)
- Total Carbohydrate: 39g carbohydrate (33g sugars

- Cholesterol: 0 cholesterol

216. Mojito

Serving: 1 | Prep: 2mins | Cook: | Ready in:

Ingredients

- 1/2 teaspoon confectioners' sugar
- 1/2 lime, juiced
- 1 sprig fresh mint, crushed
- 1/2 cup crushed ice
- 2 fluid ounces white rum
- 4 fluid ounces carbonated water
- 1 sprig fresh mint, garnish

Direction

- Stir together the lime juice and confectioners' sugar in a highball glass. Take the mint leaves to bruise and transfer into glass. Add crush ice to fill the glass, and then pour rum into glass. Fill the glass with carbonated water. Garnish by sprinkling a sprig of mint.

217. Morning Fruit Shake

Serving: 4 servings. | Prep: 10mins | Cook: 0mins | Ready in:

Ingredients

- 1 cup cranberry juice
- 2 medium ripe bananas, sliced
- 2 cups (16 ounces) raspberry yogurt or flavor of choice
- 1 tablespoon confectioners' sugar, optional
- Few drops red food coloring, optional
- Mint leaves, optional

Direction

- Mix all the ingredients in a blender. Cover the blender and blend the mixture until smooth. If desired, you can garnish the drink with mint. Pour the drink into the chilled glasses or a pitcher. Serve.

Nutrition Information

- Calories: 138 calories
- Protein: 6g protein. Diabetic Exchanges: 1 fruit
- Total Fat: 1g fat (0 saturated fat)
- Sodium: 64mg sodium
- Fiber: 0 fiber)
- Total Carbohydrate: 30g carbohydrate (0 sugars
- Cholesterol: 0 cholesterol

218. Nutty Banana Shakes

Serving: 5 servings. | Prep: 10mins | Cook: 0mins | Ready in:

Ingredients

- 1 cup milk
- 3 cups vanilla ice cream
- 4 medium ripe bananas, cut into chunks
- 1/2 cup chopped walnuts
- 4 miniature Butterfinger candy bars

Direction

- Combine all the ingredients in a blender. Cover and process the mixture until well-blended. Pour it into the chilled glasses and serve.

Nutrition Information

- Calories: 433 calories
- Protein: 10g protein.
- Total Fat: 21g fat (9g saturated fat)
- Sodium: 122mg sodium
- Fiber: 3g fiber)

- Total Carbohydrate: 56g carbohydrate (42g sugars
- Cholesterol: 42mg cholesterol

219. Old Fashioned Chocolate Malted Milk

Serving: 2 servings. | Prep: 10mins | Cook: 0mins | Ready in:

Ingredients

- 2 cups vanilla ice cream
- 2/3 cup cold milk
- 2 tablespoons malted milk powder
- 2 tablespoons chocolate syrup
- 2 to 4 tablespoons whipped cream

Direction

- Combine malted milk powder, chocolate syrup, ice cream, and milk in a blender. Cover the blender and process the mixture until smooth. Pour it into the chilled glass. Top the drink with a dollop of whipped cream. Serve.

Nutrition Information

- Calories: 443 calories
- Protein: 9g protein.
- Total Fat: 20g fat (12g saturated fat)
- Sodium: 190mg sodium
- Fiber: 0 fiber)
- Total Carbohydrate: 59g carbohydrate (46g sugars
- Cholesterol: 76mg cholesterol

220. Old Fashioned Eggnog

Serving: 18 servings (about 3 quarts). | Prep: 15mins | Cook: 25mins | Ready in:

Ingredients

- 12 eggs
- 1-1/2 cups sugar
- 1/2 teaspoon salt
- 2 quarts milk, divided
- 2 tablespoons vanilla extract
- 1 teaspoon ground nutmeg
- 2 cups heavy whipping cream
- Whipped cream and additional nutmeg, optional

Direction

- In the pot mix the sugar, salt, and eggs. Then slowly pour in 1 quart milk and stir. Reduce the heat; stir and cook on low heat until thermometer registers 160°F, 25 minutes. Transfer it into a bowl; add in the remaining milk, vanilla, and nutmeg. Put in a bath of ice water. Stir it from time to time until it cools down. If the mixture starts to separate, blend it in a food processor or blender until it smoothens. Put cover on and chill for 3 or more hours.
- In a bowl whisk cream until soft peaks appear, then gently mix into the chilled mixture. Serve in a chilled 5-quart punch bowl. Garnish with nutmeg and spoonsful of whipped cream.

Nutrition Information

- Calories: 268 calories
- Sodium: 182mg sodium
- Fiber: 0 fiber)
- Total Carbohydrate: 24g carbohydrate (0 sugars
- Cholesterol: 186mg cholesterol
- Protein: 9g protein.
- Total Fat: 15g fat (9g saturated fat)

221. Old Fashioned Ice Cream Soda

Serving: 4 servings. | Prep: 5mins | Cook: 0mins | Ready in:

Ingredients

- 1 bottle (1 liter) club soda or ginger ale
- 1 pint ice cream

Direction

- Place a 1/2 cup of club soda in each of the four tall glasses. Add a 1/2 cup of ice cream into each glass. Fill each glass with the soda. Serve.

Nutrition Information

- Calories:
- Sodium:
- Fiber:
- Total Carbohydrate:
- Cholesterol:
- Protein:
- Total Fat:

222. Orange & Coffee Martini

Serving: 1 serving. | Prep: 5mins | Cook: 0mins | Ready in:

Ingredients

- Ice cubes
- 2 ounces strong brewed coffee, cooled
- 1 ounce vodka
- 1/2 ounce orange liqueur
- 1/2 ounce hazelnut liqueur

Direction

- Fill 3/4 of a tumbler or a mixing glass with ice cubes. Stir in the leftover ingredients till condensation forms on the glass's outer side. In a chilled cocktail glass, strain the drink then immediately serve.

Nutrition Information

- Calories: 172 calories
- Protein: 0 protein.
- Total Fat: 0 fat (0 saturated fat)
- Sodium: 2mg sodium
- Fiber: 0 fiber)
- Total Carbohydrate: 13g carbohydrate (12g sugars
- Cholesterol: 0 cholesterol

223. Orange Blueberry Shakes

Serving: 3 servings. | Prep: 5mins | Cook: 0mins | Ready in:

Ingredients

- 1-1/4 cups strawberry ice cream
- 3/4 cup vanilla ice cream
- 2/3 cup orange juice
- 1-1/4 cups frozen unsweetened blueberries
- 2 teaspoons sugar
- Fresh strawberries, optional

Direction

- Mix the first five ingredients in a blender. Cover the blender and process the mixture until smooth. You can stir the mixture if needed. Pour it into the chilled glasses. If desired, garnish the drink with strawberries.

Nutrition Information

- Calories: 240 calories
- Protein: 3g protein.
- Total Fat: 9g fat (5g saturated fat)
- Sodium: 60mg sodium
- Fiber: 2g fiber)

- Total Carbohydrate: 39g carbohydrate (20g sugars
- Cholesterol: 30mg cholesterol

224. Orange Blush

Serving: 6 cups. | Prep: 5mins | Cook: 0mins | Ready in:

Ingredients

- 1 can (12 ounces) frozen orange juice concentrate, thawed
- 2 cups cranberry juice
- 1/2 cup sugar
- 1 liter club soda, chilled
- Crushed ice

Direction

- Mix together sugar, cranberry juice and orange juice concentrate in a big bowl or pitcher. Chill for a minimum of an hour. Stir in soda right before serving and serve over ice.

Nutrition Information

- Calories: 193 calories
- Sodium: 39mg sodium
- Fiber: 1g fiber)
- Total Carbohydrate: 49g carbohydrate (48g sugars
- Cholesterol: 0 cholesterol
- Protein: 2g protein.
- Total Fat: 0 fat (0 saturated fat)

225. Orange Colada

Serving: 6 servings. | Prep: 10mins | Cook: 0mins | Ready in:

Ingredients

- 1 can (6 ounces) frozen orange juice concentrate, thawed
- 6 ounces frozen non-alcoholic pina colada mix
- 1 cup milk
- 2 tablespoons lemon juice
- 1-1/2 cups crushed ice
- Orange slices

Direction

- Combine the initial 4 ingredients in a blender container. Cover and blend for 30 seconds on high till smooth. Place in ice and process till blended. Pour into a chilled glass to serve. Add an orange slice for garnish. Serve at once.

Nutrition Information

- Calories: 138 calories
- Sodium: 29mg sodium
- Fiber: 0 fiber)
- Total Carbohydrate: 27g carbohydrate (26g sugars
- Cholesterol: 6mg cholesterol
- Protein: 2g protein.
- Total Fat: 3g fat (2g saturated fat)

226. Orange Pineapple Punch

Serving: Yield: 2 quarts. | Prep: 10mins | Cook: 0mins | Ready in:

Ingredients

- 1 envelope unsweetened orange Kool-Aid mix
- 1 cup sugar
- 2 cups pineapple juice, chilled
- 3 cups cold water
- 2 cups ginger ale or lemon-lime soda, chilled

Direction

- Blend pineapple juice, sugar and Kool-Aid mix in a blender till the mixture is frothy and sugar dissolves. Transfer into a punch bowl then pour in soda and water. Serve at once.

Nutrition Information

- Calories:
- Sodium:
- Fiber:
- Total Carbohydrate:
- Cholesterol:
- Protein:
- Total Fat:

227. Orange Pineapple Smoothies

Serving: 6 servings. | Prep: 10mins | Cook: 0mins | Ready in:

Ingredients

- 1 package (16 ounces) frozen pineapple chunks
- 1 cup thawed orange juice concentrate
- 2 cans (5-1/2 ounces each) apricot nectar
- 2 cups ice cubes
- 1 envelope unsweetened orange Kool-Aid mix

Direction

- In a blender, add half of each ingredient, then cover and blend until smooth. Transfer into cold glasses. Repeat. Serve promptly.

Nutrition Information

- Calories: 155 calories
- Total Carbohydrate: 37g carbohydrate (31g sugars
- Cholesterol: 0 cholesterol
- Protein: 1g protein.
- Total Fat: 0 fat (0 saturated fat)
- Sodium: 28mg sodium
- Fiber: 1g fiber)

228. Orange Slush

Serving: 2 | Prep: 5mins | Cook: | Ready in:

Ingredients

- 1 (6 ounce) can frozen orange juice concentrate
- 1 1/2 cups milk
- 1/2 cup sugar
- 1 teaspoon vanilla extract
- 10 cubes ice

Direction

- Mix ice cubes, vanilla, sugar, milk and orange juice concentrate in a blender. Blend until smooth then transfer into glasses to serve.

Nutrition Information

- Calories: 461 calories;
- Total Fat: 3.8
- Sodium: 82
- Total Carbohydrate: 99.5
- Cholesterol: 15
- Protein: 8.6

229. Orange Soy Milk Frappes

Serving: 2 servings. | Prep: 10mins | Cook: 0mins | Ready in:

Ingredients

- 1/2 cup vanilla soy milk
- 1/2 cup orange juice
- 5 ice cubes
- 2 teaspoons sugar
- 1/4 teaspoon vanilla extract
- Dash salt

Direction

- Mix all ingredients in a blender, then cover and blend until smooth, about 30 to 45 seconds. Transfer into cold glasses and serve promptly.

Nutrition Information

- Calories: 70 calories
- Sodium: 98mg sodium
- Fiber: 0 fiber)
- Total Carbohydrate: 13g carbohydrate (11g sugars
- Cholesterol: 0 cholesterol
- Protein: 2g protein. Diabetic Exchanges: 1/2 starch
- Total Fat: 1g fat (0 saturated fat)

230. Orange Strawberry Smoothies

Serving: 6 servings. | Prep: 5mins | Cook: 0mins | Ready in:

Ingredients

- 2-1/4 cups orange juice
- 1 package (12.3 ounces) silken reduced-fat firm tofu
- 3 cups halved frozen unsweetened strawberries
- 1-1/2 cups sliced ripe bananas

Direction

- Mix together bananas, strawberries, tofu and orange juice in a food processor, then cover and process until blended. Transfer into cold glasses and serve promptly.

Nutrition Information

- Calories: 120 calories
- Protein: 5g protein. Diabetic Exchanges: 1-1/2 fruit
- Total Fat: 1g fat (0 saturated fat)
- Sodium: 51mg sodium
- Fiber: 3g fiber)
- Total Carbohydrate: 25g carbohydrate (19g sugars
- Cholesterol: 0 cholesterol

231. Orange Peach Thirst Quencher

Serving: 4 servings. | Prep: 10mins | Cook: 0mins | Ready in:

Ingredients

- 2 cups orange-tangerine juice, chilled
- 1 cup carbonated water, chilled
- 1 tablespoon honey
- 1-1/2 teaspoons lemon juice
- 1 can (14-1/2 ounces) no-sugar-added sliced peaches, drained

Direction

- Combine all of the ingredients in a blender. Cover and blend till smooth. Transfer into chilled glasses.

Nutrition Information

- Calories: 106 calories
- Sodium: 16mg sodium
- Fiber: 1g fiber)
- Total Carbohydrate: 27g carbohydrate (25g sugars
- Cholesterol: 0 cholesterol
- Protein: 0 protein. Diabetic Exchanges: 1-1/2 fruit.
- Total Fat: 0 fat (0 saturated fat)

232. Paper Crafter's Punch

Serving: 13-15 servings (2-1/2 quarts). | Prep: 10mins | Cook: 0mins | Ready in:

Ingredients

- 1 bottle (64 ounces) cranberry juice, chilled
- 1 cup orange juice, chilled
- 2 cups lemon-lime or club soda, chilled
- Orange and lime slices

Direction

- In 2 large pitchers, place the juices then add 1 cup of soda to each and stir. If desires, place in ice then add in lime and orange slices. Serve at once.

Nutrition Information

- Calories:
- Protein:
- Total Fat:
- Sodium:
- Fiber:
- Total Carbohydrate:
- Cholesterol:

233. Party Punch

Serving: about 24 servings. | Prep: 15mins | Cook: 0mins | Ready in:

Ingredients

- 3 cups warm water
- 2 cups sugar
- 3 ripe bananas, sliced
- 1 can (46 ounces) pineapple juice
- 1-1/2 cups orange juice
- 1/4 cup lemon juice
- 3 quarts ginger ale, chilled

Direction

- Combine bananas, sugar and water in a food processor. Cover and blend till smooth. Transfer into a large container. Pour in lemon juice, orange juice and pineapple juice then stir. Store in the freezer till slushy, stir occasionally. Place into a large punch bowl, add in ginger ale and stir. Serve at once.

Nutrition Information

- Calories: 157 calories
- Total Fat: 0 fat (0 saturated fat)
- Sodium: 9mg sodium
- Fiber: 0 fiber)
- Total Carbohydrate: 40g carbohydrate (38g sugars
- Cholesterol: 0 cholesterol
- Protein: 0 protein.

234. Peach Breakfast Slush

Serving: 6 servings. | Prep: 10mins | Cook: 0mins | Ready in:

Ingredients

- 1 can (15-1/4 ounces) sliced peaches, drained
- 1 can (6 ounces) frozen orange juice concentrate
- 1-1/2 cups apricot nectar
- 2 cups lemon-lime soda, chilled

Direction

- Mix together nectar, orange juice concentrate and peaches in a blender. Cover and blend until smooth.
- Transfer into a freezer container, then cover and place in the freezer until solid. To serve, scoop into a glass with 2/3 cup frozen mixture then pour in 1/3 cup soda.

Nutrition Information

- Calories:
- Cholesterol:
- Protein:
- Total Fat:
- Sodium:
- Fiber:
- Total Carbohydrate:

235. Peach Smoothie

Serving: 4 | Prep: 1mins | Cook: | Ready in:

Ingredients

- 1 (15 ounce) can sliced peaches, drained
- 4 scoops vanilla ice cream
- 2 cups vanilla soy milk
- 1/4 cup orange juice

Direction

- Mix together orange juice, soy milk, ice cream and peaches in a blender. Process until smooth then transfer into glasses and serve.

Nutrition Information

- Calories: 152 calories;
- Total Fat: 4.2
- Sodium: 75
- Total Carbohydrate: 24.8
- Cholesterol: 9
- Protein: 4.8

236. Peach Smoothies

Serving: 4 servings. | Prep: 5mins | Cook: 0mins | Ready in:

Ingredients

- 2 cups milk
- 2 cups frozen unsweetened sliced peaches
- 1/4 cup orange juice concentrate
- 2 tablespoons sugar
- 5 ice cubes

Direction

- Combine all of the ingredients in a blender; cover and blend till smooth. Transfer into chilled glasses and serve at once.

Nutrition Information

- Calories: 143 calories
- Protein: 5g protein. Diabetic Exchanges: 1 fruit
- Total Fat: 4g fat (3g saturated fat)
- Sodium: 60mg sodium
- Fiber: 2g fiber)
- Total Carbohydrate: 23g carbohydrate (21g sugars
- Cholesterol: 17mg cholesterol

237. Peach Wine Coolers

Serving: 9 servings. | Prep: 15mins | Cook: 0mins | Ready in:

Ingredients

- 2 cups frozen unsweetened sliced peaches, thawed
- 1/2 cup brandy
- 1/3 cup honey
- 1/2 lemon, very thinly sliced
- 1 bottle (750 milliliters) dry white wine
- 1-1/2 cups carbonated water, chilled
- Ice cubes

Direction

- Combine lemon slices, honey, brandy and peach slices in a 2-quart pitcher. Add in wine and stir. Store in the fridge to chill for 2-4 hours.

- Add in sparkling water and stir right before serving. Pour over ice to serve.

Nutrition Information

- Calories: 151 calories
- Total Carbohydrate: 16g carbohydrate (14g sugars
- Cholesterol: 0 cholesterol
- Protein: 0 protein.
- Total Fat: 0 fat (0 saturated fat)
- Sodium: 5mg sodium
- Fiber: 1g fiber)

238. Peachy Berry Shakes

Serving: 4 servings. | Prep: 10mins | Cook: 0mins | Ready in:

Ingredients

- 1/2 cup milk
- 3 cups vanilla ice cream
- 1-1/2 cups fresh or frozen sliced peeled peaches
- 1 cup fresh or frozen strawberries
- 3/4 cup vanilla, peach or strawberry yogurt
- Whipped cream, slivered almonds and whole fresh strawberries

Direction

- Combine strawberries, yogurt, milk, peaches, and ice cream in a blender. Cover and process it until smooth. Pour the drink into the chilled glasses. Before serving, garnish the glass with whipped cream, strawberries, and almonds. Immediately serve.

Nutrition Information

- Calories: 302 calories
- Sodium: 124mg sodium
- Fiber: 2g fiber)

- Total Carbohydrate: 41g carbohydrate (32g sugars
- Cholesterol: 52mg cholesterol
- Protein: 7g protein.
- Total Fat: 14g fat (8g saturated fat)

239. Peachy Buttermilk Shakes

Serving: 3 servings. | Prep: 10mins | Cook: 0mins | Ready in:

Ingredients

- 1 cup buttermilk
- 3 cups fresh or frozen unsweetened sliced peaches, thawed
- 1 cup vanilla ice cream, softened
- 1/4 cup sugar
- 3/4 teaspoon ground cinnamon

Direction

- Combine all the ingredients in a blender. Cover the blender and process the mixture until smooth. Pour it into the chilled glasses and serve.

Nutrition Information

- Calories:
- Total Fat:
- Sodium:
- Fiber:
- Total Carbohydrate:
- Cholesterol:
- Protein:

240. Peachy Lemonade

Serving: About 2-1/2 quarts. | Prep: 10mins | Cook: 0mins | Ready in:

Ingredients

- 8 cups lemonade
- 2 cans (5-1/2 ounces each) peach nectar or apricot nectar
- 1 cup frozen unsweetened sliced peaches
- Fresh mint sprigs, snapdragons and lemon balm

Direction

- Mix nectar and lemonade in a 3-qt glass pitcher. Chill until cold. Whisk the lemonade mixture right before serving then add in frozen peach pieces. Put along sides of the pitcher with mint sprigs and top off the lemonade with flowers to float.

Nutrition Information

- Calories: 115 calories
- Protein: 0 protein.
- Total Fat: 0 fat (0 saturated fat)
- Sodium: 15mg sodium
- Fiber: 1g fiber)
- Total Carbohydrate: 29g carbohydrate (27g sugars
- Cholesterol: 0 cholesterol

241. Peachy Strawberry Smoothie

Serving: 4 servings. | Prep: 5mins | Cook: 0mins | Ready in:

Ingredients

- 2 cups peach or apricot nectar
- 2 cups (16 ounces) plain yogurt
- 1 medium peach, peeled and sliced
- 6 frozen whole strawberries
- 2 teaspoons sugar
- 1/8 teaspoon ground cinnamon

Direction

- Mix all ingredients in a blender then cover and blend until combined, about 30 to 45 seconds. Transfer into cold glasses and serve promptly.

Nutrition Information

- Calories: 166 calories
- Cholesterol: 16mg cholesterol
- Protein: 5g protein.
- Total Fat: 4g fat (3g saturated fat)
- Sodium: 65mg sodium
- Fiber: 2g fiber)
- Total Carbohydrate: 29g carbohydrate (27g sugars

242. Peanut Butter & Banana Smoothie

Serving: 1 serving. | Prep: 10mins | Cook: 0mins | Ready in:

Ingredients

- 1/2 cup plain yogurt
- 1 medium ripe banana
- 2 tablespoons nonfat dry milk powder
- 1 tablespoon honey
- 1 tablespoon creamy peanut butter
- 2 ice cubes

Direction

- Mix all ingredients in a blender, then cover and blend until smooth, about 30 to 40 seconds. Stir if needed. Transfer into a cold glass and serve promptly.

Nutrition Information

- Calories: 393 calories
- Sodium: 214mg sodium
- Fiber: 4g fiber)
- Total Carbohydrate: 61g carbohydrate (47g sugars

- Cholesterol: 19mg cholesterol
- Protein: 15g protein.
- Total Fat: 13g fat (4g saturated fat)

243. Peanut Butter 'n' Jelly Breakfast Shake

Serving: 2 servings (2-1/2 cups). | Prep: 10mins | Cook: 0mins | Ready in:

Ingredients

- 2 cups cold milk
- 1 ripe banana, sliced
- 2 tablespoons peanut butter
- 2 tablespoons jam, jelly or preserves (any flavor)
- 1/2 teaspoon vanilla extract

Direction

- Combine all the ingredients in a blender and cover it. Blend it for 3 minutes or until smooth. Pour the mixture into the chilled glasses; serve.

Nutrition Information

- Calories: 346 calories
- Total Carbohydrate: 41g carbohydrate (32g sugars
- Cholesterol: 24mg cholesterol
- Protein: 13g protein.
- Total Fat: 16g fat (6g saturated fat)
- Sodium: 173mg sodium
- Fiber: 2g fiber)

244. Pear Cooler

Serving: 3 servings. | Prep: 5mins | Cook: 0mins | Ready in:

Ingredients

- 1 can (15-1/4 ounces) sliced pears, undrained
- 2 cups ice cubes
- 1 envelope whipped topping mix (Dream Whip)
- 1/4 to 1/2 teaspoon vanilla or almond extract, optional

Direction

- Combine all of the ingredients in a blender. Cover and blend till smooth. Transfer into chilled glasses and serve at once.

Nutrition Information

- Calories: 165 calories
- Sodium: 11mg sodium
- Fiber: 1g fiber)
- Total Carbohydrate: 33g carbohydrate (32g sugars
- Cholesterol: 0 cholesterol
- Protein: 1g protein.
- Total Fat: 2g fat (2g saturated fat)

245. Pear Slushy

Serving: 2 servings. | Prep: 5mins | Cook: 0mins | Ready in:

Ingredients

- 1 cup chopped peeled ripe pear
- 1/4 cup orange juice
- 1/4 cup unsweetened pineapple juice
- 2 tablespoons honey
- 6 ice cubes

Direction

- Mix all ingredients in a blender, then cover and blend until smooth. Transfer into cold glasses and serve promptly.

Nutrition Information

- Calories: 144 calories
- Sodium: 2mg sodium
- Fiber: 2g fiber)
- Total Carbohydrate: 37g carbohydrate (32g sugars
- Cholesterol: 0 cholesterol
- Protein: 1g protein.
- Total Fat: 0 fat (0 saturated fat)

246. Pennsylvania Milk Punch

Serving: 20 servings. | Prep: 15mins | Cook: 0mins | Ready in:

Ingredients

- 4 cups milk
- 1 quart orange sherbet, softened
- 1 pint vanilla ice cream, softened
- 1 liter lemon-lime soda

Direction

- Beat ice cream, sherbet and milk in a bowl till frothy. Transfer into a punch bowl. Add soda and stir. Serve at once.

Nutrition Information

- Calories: 91 calories
- Fiber: 0 fiber)
- Total Carbohydrate: 18g carbohydrate (0 sugars
- Cholesterol: 3mg cholesterol
- Protein: 3g protein. Diabetic Exchanges: 1 starch.
- Total Fat: 1g fat (0 saturated fat)
- Sodium: 61mg sodium

247. Peppermint Eggnog Punch

Serving: 16 | Prep: 10mins | Cook: | Ready in:

Ingredients

- 1 quart peppermint ice cream
- 1 quart eggnog
- 4 (12 fluid ounce) cans or bottles ginger ale, chilled
- 1 cup rum
- 24 small peppermint candy canes for garnish

Direction

- Freeze 2 or 3 scoops of ice cream and set aside for finishing touches. Mix the remaining ice cream until it is soft. Mix in rum and eggnog slowly. Put the mixture into a punch bowl then mix ginger ale in. Decorate the punch bowl with candy canes by hanging them around the edges. Let the frozen ice cream scoops float on top and serve right away.

Nutrition Information

- Calories: 380 calories;
- Total Carbohydrate: 65.1
- Cholesterol: 52
- Protein: 3.6
- Total Fat: 8.4
- Sodium: 87

248. Picnic Fruit Punch

Serving: 5 quarts. | Prep: 10mins | Cook: 0mins | Ready in:

Ingredients

- 8 cups cranberry juice
- 3 cups pineapple juice
- 3 cups orange juice
- 1/4 cup lemon juice

- 1 liter ginger ale, chilled
- 1 medium navel orange, sliced

Direction

- Mix juices in a big container and chill. Right before serving, turn to a punch bowl and stir in orange slices and ginger ale.

Nutrition Information

- Calories: 106 calories
- Total Fat: 0 fat (0 saturated fat)
- Sodium: 6mg sodium
- Fiber: 0 fiber)
- Total Carbohydrate: 27g carbohydrate (26g sugars
- Cholesterol: 0 cholesterol
- Protein: 1g protein.

249. Pineapple Cooler

Serving: 2-2/3 cups. | Prep: 5mins | Cook: 0mins | Ready in:

Ingredients

- 1 cup unsweetened pineapple juice, chilled
- 1 to 2 tablespoons lemon juice
- 1 can (12 ounces) lemon-lime soda, chilled
- Ice cubes

Direction

- In a pitcher, combine all of the ingredients then pour over ice to serve.

Nutrition Information

- Calories: 48 calories
- Total Fat: 0 fat (0 saturated fat)
- Sodium: 13mg sodium
- Fiber: 0 fiber)

- Total Carbohydrate: 12g carbohydrate (0 sugars
- Cholesterol: 0 cholesterol
- Protein: 0 protein. Diabetic Exchanges: 1 fruit.

250. Pineapple Orange Slush

Serving: 2 servings. | Prep: 10mins | Cook: 0mins | Ready in:

Ingredients

- 1 cup orange juice
- 1/2 cup unsweetened pineapple juice
- 2 tablespoons lemon juice
- 2 cups crushed ice cubes

Direction

- Mix all ingredients in a blender then cover and blend until slushy and thick. Transfer into cold glasses and serve promptly.

Nutrition Information

- Calories: 95 calories
- Sodium: 2mg sodium
- Fiber: 0 fiber)
- Total Carbohydrate: 23g carbohydrate (0 sugars
- Cholesterol: 0 cholesterol
- Protein: 1g protein. Diabetic Exchanges: 1-1/2 fruit.
- Total Fat: 0 fat (0 saturated fat)

251. Pineapple Punch

Serving: Makes about 30 cups | Prep: | Cook: | Ready in:

Ingredients

- 1 large ripe pineapple (4 1/4lb) (preferably "extra sweet")
- 2 750-ml bottles dry white wine
- 1/2 cup brandy
- 1/4 cup confectioners sugar
- 1 cup granulated sugar
- 1 cup water
- 2 chilled 750-ml bottles Champagne
- a candy thermometer

Direction

- Chop off and throw away the top of the pineapple. Chop off the rind and slice it into 2-in. pieces. Slice the pineapple lengthwise into quarters and chop away the core, and then slice the core into 2-in. pieces. In a food processor, process the core and rind into a coarse purée, working in batches if needed.
- In a bowl, put the pineapple purée and mix in white wine. Cover and refrigerate for 60 minutes.
- Slice the leftover pineapple into 1/3-in. dice and mix with confectioners' sugar and brandy in a separate bowl. Cover and refrigerate to macerate for 60 minutes, tossing sometimes.
- As the pineapple macerates, boil water and granulated sugar, whisking until the sugar dissolves, and then boil the syrup over moderate heat without stirring until a candy thermometer displays 230°F. Let the syrup cool.
- Transfer the wine mixture into a punch bowl set in cracked ice through a big fine sieve and mix in Champagne, pineapple with liquid and syrup.

Nutrition Information

- Calories: 514
- Total Carbohydrate: 55 g(18%)
- Protein: 1 g(2%)
- Total Fat: 0 g(1%)
- Saturated Fat: 0 g(1%)
- Sodium: 22 mg(1%)
- Fiber: 2 g(7%)

252. Pineapple Sunrise Smoothies

Serving: 2 servings. | Prep: 5mins | Cook: 0mins | Ready in:

Ingredients

- 1 can (14 ounces) unsweetened pineapple tidbits
- 1 small ripe banana, sliced
- 3/4 cup fresh or frozen raspberries
- 2 tablespoons sugar
- 2 ice cubes

Direction

- Drain pineapple, saving 1 cup pineapple and juice (chill the leftover pineapple for another use.) Mix together ice, sugar, raspberries, banana, pineapple and pineapple juice in blender then cover and blend until smooth. Stir if needed. Transfer into cold glasses and serve promptly.

Nutrition Information

- Calories: 205 calories
- Protein: 1g protein.
- Total Fat: 1g fat (0 saturated fat)
- Sodium: 18mg sodium
- Fiber: 6g fiber)
- Total Carbohydrate: 56g carbohydrate (0 sugars
- Cholesterol: 0 cholesterol

253. Pink Grapefruit Punch

Serving: 8-10 servings (1-3/4 quarts). | Prep: 5mins | Cook: 0mins | Ready in:

Ingredients

- 4 cups water, divided
- 2 tablespoons confectioners' sugar
- 2 cups pink grapefruit juice
- 1 can (12 ounces) frozen pink lemonade concentrate, thawed
- 3 tablespoons maraschino cherry juice
- Orange or lemon slices and maraschino cherries, optional

Direction

- In a small microwavable bowl, mix sugar and 1/4 cup water. Microwave for a half minute on high, until sugar is dissolved. Let it cool. Mix the leftover water, sugar mixture, cherry juice, lemonade concentrate and grapefruit juice in a big pitcher. Refrigerate. Serve over ice and decorate with lemon or orange slices and cherries if you want.

Nutrition Information

- Calories: 89 calories
- Protein: 0 protein.
- Total Fat: 0 fat (0 saturated fat)
- Sodium: 2mg sodium
- Fiber: 0 fiber)
- Total Carbohydrate: 23g carbohydrate (21g sugars
- Cholesterol: 0 cholesterol

254. Pink Party Punch

Serving: 32 servings (6 quarts). | Prep: 10mins | Cook: 0mins | Ready in:

Ingredients

- 2 bottles (46 ounces each) white grape juice, chilled
- 1 bottle (48 ounces) cranberry juice, chilled
- 2 cans (12 ounces each) frozen lemonade concentrate, thawed
- 1 bottle (1 liter) club soda, chilled
- 2 cups lemon sherbet or sorbet

Direction

- Combine lemonade concentrate and juices in 2 pitchers and store in the fridge till serving.
- Add club soda, stir and place scoops of sherbet on top just before serving.

Nutrition Information

- Calories: 127 calories
- Sodium: 16mg sodium
- Fiber: 0 fiber)
- Total Carbohydrate: 31g carbohydrate (30g sugars
- Cholesterol: 0 cholesterol
- Protein: 1g protein.
- Total Fat: 0 fat (0 saturated fat)

255. Pink Sparkling Wine Punch

Serving: 18 servings (3/4 cup each). | Prep: 20mins | Cook: 0mins | Ready in:

Ingredients

- 2 cups fresh strawberries, hulled
- 3 tablespoons lemon juice
- 3 tablespoons honey
- 2 bottles (32 ounces each) cranberry juice, chilled
- 1 cup cold water
- 3/4 cup thawed pink lemonade concentrate
- 1 bottle (750 milliliters) sparkling rose wine, chilled
- Thinly sliced strawberries, lemons and limes

Direction

- In a food processor, place honey, lemon juice and strawberries then blend till pureed. If preferred, through a fine-mesh strainer, press the mixture into a punch bowl and remove

seeds. Add in lemonade concentrate, water and cranberry juice then stir.
- Add in wine and stir right before serving. Add sliced fruit to serve.

Nutrition Information

- Calories:
- Sodium:
- Fiber:
- Total Carbohydrate:
- Cholesterol:
- Protein:
- Total Fat:

256. Poinsettia

Serving: 1 serving. | Prep: 5mins | Cook: 0mins | Ready in:

Ingredients

- 1 ounce cranberry juice
- 1/2 ounce Triple Sec, optional
- 4 ounces chilled Champagne or other sparkling wine
- GARNISH:
- 3 fresh cranberries

Direction

- In a wine glass or a champagne flute, add cranberry juice and (if desired) Triple Sec. Pour Champagne on top. Garnish as preferred.

Nutrition Information

- Calories: 95 calories
- Protein: 0 protein.
- Total Fat: 0 fat (0 saturated fat)
- Sodium: 7mg sodium
- Fiber: 0 fiber)
- Total Carbohydrate: 5g carbohydrate (4g sugars
- Cholesterol: 0 cholesterol

257. Pomegranate Champagne Cocktail

Serving: 1 serving. | Prep: 5mins | Cook: 0mins | Ready in:

Ingredients

- 1 sugar cube or 1 teaspoon sugar
- 2 to 4 dashes bitters, optional
- 1 ounce pomegranate juice
- 1/2 ounce brandy
- 1/2 ounce pomegranate liqueur
- 1/3 cup Champagne
- GARNISH:
- Pomegranate seeds

Direction

- In a champagne flute, place sugar and drizzle with bitters if preferred. Pour liqueur, brandy and juice into the glass. Add Champagne on top. Place in pomegranate seeds for garnish.

Nutrition Information

- Calories: 126 calories
- Total Fat: 0 fat (0 saturated fat)
- Sodium: 4mg sodium
- Fiber: 0 fiber)
- Total Carbohydrate: 8g carbohydrate (7g sugars
- Cholesterol: 0 cholesterol
- Protein: 0 protein.

258. Pomegranate Ginger Spritzer

Serving: 7 cups. | Prep: 10mins | Cook: 0mins | Ready in:

Ingredients

- 1/2 cup sliced fresh gingerroot
- 1 medium lime, sliced
- 3 cups pomegranate juice
- 3/4 cup orange juice
- 3 cups chilled club soda

Direction

- In a pitcher, place slices of lime and ginger. Add in orange juices and pomegranate, stir. Store in the fridge overnight.
- Strain and remove lime and ginger right before serving. Add club soda into the juice mixture and stir.

Nutrition Information

- Calories: 80 calories
- Protein: 1g protein. Diabetic Exchanges: 1 fruit.
- Total Fat: 0 fat (0 saturated fat)
- Sodium: 35mg sodium
- Fiber: 0 fiber)
- Total Carbohydrate: 20g carbohydrate (17g sugars
- Cholesterol: 0 cholesterol

259. Pretty Pink Punch

Serving: 50 servings (7-1/2 quarts). | Prep: 15mins | Cook: 0mins | Ready in:

Ingredients

- 2 tablespoons sugar
- 3 cups cold water
- 2 bottles (64 ounces each) cranberry-raspberry juice, chilled
- 1 can (46 ounces) pineapple juice, chilled
- 1 can (12 ounces) frozen pink lemonade concentrate, thawed
- 1 liter ginger ale, chilled
- Decorative ice mold & lemon slices, optional

Direction

- Let sugar dissolve in a punch bowl of water. Mix lemonade and juices well. Add in ginger ale and stir. Place lemon slices and a decorative ice mold on top if preferred. Serve at once.

Nutrition Information

- Calories: 76 calories
- Protein: 0 protein.
- Total Fat: 0 fat (0 saturated fat)
- Sodium: 5mg sodium
- Fiber: 0 fiber)
- Total Carbohydrate: 19g carbohydrate (18g sugars
- Cholesterol: 0 cholesterol

260. Pumpkin Patch Punch

Serving: 12 servings. | Prep: 15mins | Cook: 0mins | Ready in:

Ingredients

- 4 medium lemons
- 4 medium limes
- 4 medium oranges
- 3 quarts water
- 1-1/2 to 2 cups sugar
- Additional oranges and lime peel

Direction

- Squeeze juice from oranges, limes and lemons into a gallon container. Add in sugar and water then mix well. Store in the fridge to chill.
- For making pumpkins, cut the bottom and top thirds from the amount of oranges you desire. Use a paring knife to insert a small lime peel piece on a pumpkin steam.

- Right before serving, pour the punch into serving pitchers and place in ice if preferred. Place pumpkin on top of each serving.

Nutrition Information

- Calories:
- Sodium:
- Fiber:
- Total Carbohydrate:
- Cholesterol:
- Protein:
- Total Fat:

261. Purple Cows

Serving: 4 servings. | Prep: 10mins | Cook: 0mins | Ready in:

Ingredients

- 1-1/2 cups milk
- 3/4 cup thawed grape juice concentrate
- 2 cups vanilla ice cream

Direction

- Mix grape juice concentrate and milk in a blender. Add the ice cream. Cover and blend the mixture until smooth. Serve.

Nutrition Information

- Calories: 286 calories
- Cholesterol: 41mg cholesterol
- Protein: 6g protein.
- Total Fat: 10g fat (6g saturated fat)
- Sodium: 101mg sodium
- Fiber: 0 fiber)
- Total Carbohydrate: 44g carbohydrate (16g sugars

262. Purple People Eater Punch

Serving: 16 | Prep: 5mins | Cook: | Ready in:

Ingredients

- 1 plastic witch's cauldron (from party store)
- 1 pint grape sherbet, softened
- 2 (2 liter) bottles grape soda
- 1 pound dry ice

Direction

- In serving area, set up the cauldron and stir grape soda and grape sherbet together in it till smooth. Use tongs to carefully place in dry ice. It may sink into the bottom and make the punch bubble and smoke. Dry ice is so cold that it can burn if ingested or touched so be careful. Don't consume dry ice.

Nutrition Information

- Calories: 112 calories;
- Total Carbohydrate: 29.1
- Cholesterol: 0
- Protein: 0
- Total Fat: 0
- Sodium: 39

263. Quick Cranberry Fruit Punch

Serving: 24 servings (about 4 quarts) | Prep: 10mins | Cook: 0mins | Ready in:

Ingredients

- 5 cups cranberry juice, chilled
- 5 cups white grape juice, chilled
- 5 cups pineapple juice, chilled
- 3 cups ginger ale, chilled
- 1 pint orange sherbet

Direction

- In a punch bowl, combine ginger ale and juices just before serving. Scoop in sherbet.

Nutrition Information

- Calories: 112 calories
- Fiber: 0 fiber)
- Total Carbohydrate: 27g carbohydrate (26g sugars
- Cholesterol: 1mg cholesterol
- Protein: 1g protein.
- Total Fat: 0 fat (0 saturated fat)
- Sodium: 12mg sodium

264. Quick Watermelon Cooler

Serving: 4 servings. | Prep: 10mins | Cook: 0mins | Ready in:

Ingredients

- 2 cups lemonade
- 3 cups seedless watermelon, coarsely chopped
- 1 cup crushed ice

Direction

- Mix all ingredients in a blender, then cover and blend until smooth. Transfer into cold glasses and serve promptly.

Nutrition Information

- Calories: 86 calories
- Sodium: 12mg sodium
- Fiber: 1g fiber)
- Total Carbohydrate: 24g carbohydrate (22g sugars
- Cholesterol: 0 cholesterol
- Protein: 0 protein. Diabetic Exchanges: 1 starch
- Total Fat: 0 fat (0 saturated fat)

265. Quick White Sangria

Serving: 6 servings. | Prep: 15mins | Cook: 0mins | Ready in:

Ingredients

- 1/4 cup sugar
- 1/4 cup brandy
- 1 cup sliced peeled fresh or frozen peaches, thawed
- 1 cup sliced fresh or frozen sliced strawberries, thawed
- 1 medium lemon, sliced
- 1 medium lime, sliced
- 1 bottle (750 milliliters) dry white wine, chilled
- 1 can (12 ounces) lemon-lime soda, chilled
- Ice cubes

Direction

- Mix brandy and sugar in a pitcher till sugar dissolves. Place in the leftover ingredients and stir gently till combined. Pour over ice to serve.

Nutrition Information

- Calories: 196 calories
- Sodium: 12mg sodium
- Fiber: 1g fiber)
- Total Carbohydrate: 23g carbohydrate (19g sugars
- Cholesterol: 0 cholesterol
- Protein: 1g protein.
- Total Fat: 0 fat (0 saturated fat)

266. Raindrop Raspberry Tea

Serving: about 2 quarts. | Prep: 15mins | Cook: 0mins | Ready in:

Ingredients

- 4 cups water
- 6 tea bags
- 3/4 to 1 cup sugar
- 4 cups cold water
- 1 cup thawed raspberry juice blend concentrate
- Ice cubes

Direction

- Boil 4 cups of water in a large saucepan. Take away from the heat and place in tea bags. Cover then let steep for 5 minutes. Remove the tea bags. Add in sugar and stir to dissolve. Pour in juice concentrate and cold water. Pour over ice in a chilled glass to serve.

Nutrition Information

- Calories: 136 calories
- Cholesterol: 0 cholesterol
- Protein: 0 protein.
- Total Fat: 0 fat (0 saturated fat)
- Sodium: 14mg sodium
- Fiber: 0 fiber)
- Total Carbohydrate: 34g carbohydrate (31g sugars

267. Raspberry Champagne Cocktail

Serving: 8 Servings | Prep: | Cook: | Ready in:

Ingredients

- 2 1/2-pint baskets fresh raspberries
- 2 tablespoons sugar
- 1/2 cup plus 2 tablespoons raspberry liqueur
- 1/4 cup cognac or other brandy
- 8 sugar cubes
- 1 750-ml bottled chilled brut champagne
- Fresh raspberries
- Lemon peel strips

Direction

- In a medium bowl, combine 2 tbsp. of sugar and 2 baskets of raspberries. Use a fork to lightly mash the berries. Allow to stand for 15 minutes. Mix in brandy and liqueur. Transfer into a jar. Cover then let stand for 3 days in a dark cupboard. Strain the raspberry mixture and use a spoon to press on the solids to extract as much liquid as you can. You can make this 1 month ahead then cover and keep chilled.
- In each of eight 6-ounce champagne flutes, place 1 sugar cube then pour over with 2 tbsp. of raspberry mixture. Fill glasses with champagne. Add lemon peel and raspberries for garnish.

268. Raspberry Cream Smoothies

Serving: 6 servings. | Prep: 10mins | Cook: 0mins | Ready in:

Ingredients

- 2 cups orange juice
- 2 cups fat-free reduced-sugar raspberry yogurt
- 2 cups frozen vanilla yogurt
- 2 small ripe bananas, cut into chunks and frozen (1 cup)
- 3 cups frozen raspberries
- 2 teaspoons vanilla extract

Direction

- Cover and blend ingredients in batches, in a food processor or a blender, until combined. Stir if needed. Transfer into cold glasses and serve promptly.

Nutrition Information

- Calories: 198 calories
- Protein: 7g protein. Diabetic Exchanges: 2 fruit
- Total Fat: 1g fat (1g saturated fat)
- Sodium: 98mg sodium
- Fiber: 2g fiber)
- Total Carbohydrate: 40g carbohydrate (0 sugars
- Cholesterol: 5mg cholesterol

269. Raspberry Mint Cooler

Serving: 3-1/2 quarts. | Prep: 20mins | Cook: 10mins | Ready in:

Ingredients

- 3 cups water
- 1 to 1-1/2 cups chopped fresh mint
- 3/4 cup sugar
- 3 packages (10 ounces each) frozen sweetened raspberries, thawed
- 2-1/4 cups lemonade concentrate
- 6 cups cold water
- Crushed ice

Direction

- Add sugar, mint and water in a big saucepan then bring mixture to a boil. Whisk in sugar until it is dissolved. Take away from heat and allow to stand about 5 minutes. Put in the lemonade concentrate and raspberries. Mash the raspberries gently.
- Use 4 layers of cheesecloth to line a strainer and put over a 1-gal container. Pour the raspberry mixture gently into the strainer to get rid of mint and pulp. Stir in the raspberry juice with cold water. Serve over ice in cold glasses.

Nutrition Information

- Calories: 149 calories
- Sodium: 3mg sodium

- Fiber: 1g fiber)
- Total Carbohydrate: 38g carbohydrate (34g sugars
- Cholesterol: 0 cholesterol
- Protein: 0 protein.
- Total Fat: 0 fat (0 saturated fat)

270. Raspberry Pomegranate Smoothies

Serving: 4 servings. | Prep: 10mins | Cook: 0mins | Ready in:

Ingredients

- 1-1/2 cups pomegranate juice
- 2 cups frozen unsweetened raspberries
- 1/4 cup packed brown sugar
- 2 cups low-fat vanilla frozen yogurt

Direction

- Mix together brown sugar, raspberries and juice in a blender. Cover and blend until combined. Put in frozen yogurt then cover and blend until blended. Transfer into cold glass and serve promptly.

Nutrition Information

- Calories: 311 calories
- Protein: 10g protein.
- Total Fat: 3g fat (1g saturated fat)
- Sodium: 61mg sodium
- Fiber: 5g fiber)
- Total Carbohydrate: 64g carbohydrate (50g sugars
- Cholesterol: 45mg cholesterol

271. Raspberry Refresher

Serving: 4 | Prep: 5mins | Cook: | Ready in:

Ingredients

- 1 liter carbonated water
- 1 pint raspberries

Direction

- In a blender or a food processor, puree the raspberries. Transfer the raspberry puree into 4 glasses. Add carbonated water to fill glasses. Place in glass with a straw to serve.

Nutrition Information

- Calories: 38 calories;
- Total Fat: 0.4
- Sodium: 7
- Total Carbohydrate: 9
- Cholesterol: 0
- Protein: 0.7

272. Raspberry Smoothies

Serving: 3 servings. | Prep: 5mins | Cook: 0mins | Ready in:

Ingredients

- 1 cup milk
- 1 cup fresh or frozen unsweetened raspberries
- 1 small ripe banana, cut into chunks
- 1/2 cup apple juice
- 1/2 cup raspberry yogurt

Direction

- Mix all ingredients in a blender then cover and blend until combined. Transfer into cold glasses and serve promptly.

Nutrition Information

- Calories: 147 calories
- Sodium: 70mg sodium
- Fiber: 4g fiber)
- Total Carbohydrate: 29g carbohydrate (0 sugars
- Cholesterol: 8mg cholesterol
- Protein: 5g protein. Diabetic Exchanges: 1 fruit
- Total Fat: 2g fat (1g saturated fat)

273. Raspberry Sweet Tea

Serving: 15 servings. | Prep: 5mins | Cook: 15mins | Ready in:

Ingredients

- 4 quarts water, divided
- Sugar substitute equivalent to 1 cup sugar
- 10 individual tea bags
- 1 package (12 ounces) frozen unsweetened raspberries, thawed and undrained
- 3 tablespoons lime juice

Direction

- Boil 2 quarts of water in a large saucepan. Add in sugar substitute and stir to dissolve. Take away from the heat.
- Place in tea bags then let steep for 5-8 minutes. Remove tea bags.
- Boil the leftover water and raspberries in a separated saucepan. Lower heat then simmer for 3 minutes, uncovered. Strain and remove the pulp. Add lime juice and raspberry juice to the tea. Pour into a large pitcher then store in the fridge to chill.

Nutrition Information

- Calories: 17 calories
- Total Carbohydrate: 4g carbohydrate (1g sugars
- Cholesterol: 0 cholesterol
- Protein: 0 protein.
- Total Fat: 0 fat (0 saturated fat)
- Sodium: 0 sodium
- Fiber: 1g fiber)

274. Red Carpet Tini

Serving: 1 serving. | Prep: 5mins | Cook: 0mins | Ready in:

Ingredients

- Ice cubes
- 1 ounce raspberry liqueur
- 1/2 ounce orange liqueur
- 1/2 ounce pomegranate juice
- 3 fresh raspberries
- 1/2 cup chilled Champagne

Direction

- Add ice to fill 1/3 of a tumbler or a mixing glass. Pour in pomegranate juice, orange liqueur and raspberry liqueur. Stir till it forms condensation on the outside of the glass.
- In a cocktail glass or a chilled champagne flute, place raspberries. Into the glass, strain the liqueur mixture then pour over the top with Champagne.

Nutrition Information

- Calories: 243 calories
- Total Carbohydrate: 20g carbohydrate (18g sugars
- Cholesterol: 0 cholesterol
- Protein: 0 protein.
- Total Fat: 0 fat (0 saturated fat)
- Sodium: 2mg sodium
- Fiber: 0 fiber)

275. Refreshing Citrus Iced Tea

Serving: 2 cups syrup (8 servings). | Prep: 15mins | Cook: 30mins | Ready in:

Ingredients

- 2-1/2 cups water
- 1/2 cup plus 2 tablespoons sugar
- 1 cup orange juice
- 3 tablespoons lemon juice
- 1 tablespoon lime juice
- 1 teaspoon grated lime zest
- ADDITIONAL INGREDIENT (for each serving):
- 3/4 cup brewed tea

Direction

- Boil sugar and water in a large saucepan. Lower heat then place in lime zest and juices. Let simmer for 30 minutes, uncovered. Strain the syrup and store in the fridge for 2 hours.

Nutrition Information

- Calories: 76 calories
- Sodium: 0 sodium
- Fiber: 0 fiber)
- Total Carbohydrate: 20g carbohydrate (18g sugars
- Cholesterol: 0 cholesterol
- Protein: 0 protein.
- Total Fat: 0 fat (0 saturated fat)

276. Refreshing Mojito

Serving: 1 serving. | Prep: 5mins | Cook: 0mins | Ready in:

Ingredients

- 2 ounces Mojito mix, divided
- 1 mint sprig
- 1/2 teaspoon sugar
- 1 to 1-1/2 cups ice cubes
- 2 ounces apple rum or light rum
- 1 ounce club soda

Direction

- In a highball glass, place sugar, mint and 1 ounce of Mojito mix. Place in ice. Pour the leftover Mojito mix, club soda and rum into the glass then stir. Serve at once.

Nutrition Information

- Calories: 190 calories
- Total Carbohydrate: 15g carbohydrate (15g sugars
- Cholesterol: 0 cholesterol
- Protein: 0 protein.
- Total Fat: 0 fat (0 saturated fat)
- Sodium: 33mg sodium
- Fiber: 0 fiber)

277. Rhubarb Cheesecake Smoothies

Serving: 6 servings. | Prep: 20mins | Cook: 0mins | Ready in:

Ingredients

- 2 cups diced fresh or frozen rhubarb
- 1/4 cup water
- 4 tablespoons honey, divided
- 1-1/2 cups vanilla ice cream
- 1 cup milk
- 1 cup frozen sweetened sliced strawberries
- 2 packages (3 ounces each) cream cheese, cubed
- 1/2 cup vanilla yogurt
- 1/4 cup confectioners' sugar
- 5 ice cubes

Direction

- Add 2 tbsp. honey, water and rhubarb in a big saucepan and bring to a boil. Lower heat then cover and simmer until rhubarb is softened, about 5-10 minutes. Take away from heat and allow to cool to room temperature.
- Mix together the leftover honey, ice cubes, icing sugar, yogurt, cream cheese, strawberries, rhubarb mixture, milk and ice cream in a blender. Cover and blend until smooth, about 1 minute. Transfer into cold glasses and serve promptly.

Nutrition Information

- Calories: 323 calories
- Cholesterol: 53mg cholesterol
- Protein: 6g protein.
- Total Fat: 16g fat (10g saturated fat)
- Sodium: 147mg sodium
- Fiber: 2g fiber)
- Total Carbohydrate: 43g carbohydrate (38g sugars

278. Rhubarb Punch

Serving: 24 servings (16 ounces each). | Prep: 10mins | Cook: 20mins | Ready in:

Ingredients

- 3 quarts diced fresh or frozen rhubarb
- 4-1/2 cups sugar
- 3 quarts water
- 1 can (6 ounces) frozen orange juice concentrate, thawed
- 3 tablespoons lemon juice
- Lemon-lime soda

Direction

- Boil water, sugar and rhubarb in a heavy saucepan. Boil for 15 minutes, then let it cool and strain. Whisk in lemon and orange juices. Let it chill. Mix together 12 oz. soda and half a cup of rhubarb syrup for each serving; pour in a chilled glass to serve.

Nutrition Information

- Calories: 329 calories
- Sodium: 39mg sodium
- Fiber: 1g fiber)
- Total Carbohydrate: 83g carbohydrate (76g sugars
- Cholesterol: 0 cholesterol
- Protein: 1g protein.
- Total Fat: 0 fat (0 saturated fat)

279. Rhubarb Slush

Serving: 20 | Prep: 10mins | Cook: 15mins | Ready in:

Ingredients

- 6 cups fresh rhubarb, chopped
- 2 cups white sugar
- 1 (6 ounce) can frozen orange juice concentrate, thawed
- 1 (6 ounce) can frozen lemonade concentrate, thawed
- 1 cup gin (optional)
- 3 cups water
- 1 (2 liter) bottle lemon-lime flavored carbonated beverage, chilled

Direction

- In a big saucepan, add rhubarb and fill water in to cover. On a medium high heat, bring to a boil and let cook until softened. Drain and use a blender to puree or mash it.
- Whisk water, gin, lemonade concentrate, orange juice concentrate, sugar and rhubarb puree together, put in the freezer. Put into serving glasses with scoops of frozen mixture, then fill lemon-lime soda in the rest of the glass.

Nutrition Information

- Calories: 193 calories;
- Total Fat: 0.1
- Sodium: 14
- Total Carbohydrate: 41.7
- Cholesterol: 0
- Protein: 0.6

280. Rock A Bye Baby Punch

Serving: about 2 gallons (about 64 half-cup servings). | Prep: 10mins | Cook: 0mins | Ready in:

Ingredients

- 3 quarts raspberry sherbet, softened
- 6 liters ginger ale, chilled

Direction

- Right before serving, in a punch bowl, place sherbet. Stir in ginger ale till sherbet almost melts.

Nutrition Information

- Calories: 71 calories
- Sodium: 20mg sodium
- Fiber: 0 fiber)
- Total Carbohydrate: 17g carbohydrate (15g sugars
- Cholesterol: 2mg cholesterol
- Protein: 0 protein.
- Total Fat: 1g fat (0 saturated fat)

281. Rosy Rhubarb Punch

Serving: 10 servings (2-1/2 quarts). | Prep: 10mins | Cook: 20mins | Ready in:

Ingredients

- 2 quarts water
- 4 cups chopped fresh or frozen rhubarb
- 2 cans (6 ounces each) unsweetened pineapple juice

- 1 cup sugar
- 2 tablespoons orange or cherry gelatin powder

Direction

- Combine rhubarb and water in a Dutch oven then boil. Lower heat then cover and let simmer till rhubarb is tender, for 10 minutes.
- Strain the mixture, save the liquid, then bring back to the pan. Add in gelatin powder, sugar and pineapple juice then stir and heat to dissolve the sugar. Let cool and pour into a pitcher or a punch bowl. Cover and store in the fridge to chill.

Nutrition Information

- Calories: 116 calories
- Protein: 1g protein.
- Total Fat: 0 fat (0 saturated fat)
- Sodium: 9mg sodium
- Fiber: 1g fiber)
- Total Carbohydrate: 29g carbohydrate (26g sugars
- Cholesterol: 0 cholesterol

282. Sangria Wine

Serving: 10 servings. | Prep: 10mins | Cook: 0mins | Ready in:

Ingredients

- 1 bottle (750 milliliters) dry red wine
- 1 cup lemon-flavored rum
- 2 cans (12 ounces each) lemon-lime soda, chilled
- 2 medium lemons, sliced
- 2 medium limes, sliced
- Ice cubes

Direction

- Combine soda, rum and wine in a pitcher. Place in lime and lemon slices. Pour over ice to serve.

Nutrition Information

- Calories: 151 calories
- Cholesterol: 0 cholesterol
- Protein: 0 protein.
- Total Fat: 0 fat (0 saturated fat)
- Sodium: 12mg sodium
- Fiber: 1g fiber)
- Total Carbohydrate: 12g carbohydrate (8g sugars

283. Santa's Orange Kissed Cocktail

Serving: 1 serving. | Prep: 5mins | Cook: 0mins | Ready in:

Ingredients

- Ice cubes
- 1/4 cup light rum
- 1/4 cup unsweetened pineapple juice
- 1 tablespoon lime juice
- 2 tablespoons orange juice
- 1 teaspoon grenadine syrup
- 3 tablespoons lemon-lime soda

Direction

- Add ice to fill 3/4 of a shaker. Pour in grenadine syrup, juices and rum.
- Cover then shake till it forms condensation on the outside of the shaker, for 10-15 seconds. In a chilled glass, strain the drink and pour soda over the top.

Nutrition Information

- Calories: 209 calories
- Fiber: 0 fiber)

- Total Carbohydrate: 20g carbohydrate (16g sugars
- Cholesterol: 0 cholesterol
- Protein: 1g protein.
- Total Fat: 0 fat (0 saturated fat)
- Sodium: 7mg sodium

284. Screwdriver

Serving: Serves 1 | Prep: | Cook: | Ready in:

Ingredients

- 1 1/2 ounces vodka
- 3 ounces orange juice
- 3 or 4 ice cubes
- Dash Angostura bitters

Direction

- In an ice-filled rocks glass, add orange juice and vodka. Stir till chilled and add a dash of bitters for garnish.

285. Sensational Slush

Serving: 20 servings. | Prep: 25mins | Cook: 0mins | Ready in:

Ingredients

- 1/2 cup sugar
- 1 package (3 ounces) strawberry gelatin
- 2 cups boiling water
- 1 cup unsweetened pineapple juice
- 2 cups sliced fresh strawberries
- 1 can (12 ounces) frozen lemonade concentrate, thawed
- 1 can (12 ounces) frozen limeade concentrate, thawed
- 2 cups cold water
- 2 liters lemon-lime soda, chilled

Direction

- Dissolve gelatin and sugar in a big bowl with boiling water. Mix strawberries and pineapple juice in a blender, then cover and blend until combined. Put in the gelatin mixture, then stir in cold water and concentrates. Cover and place in the freezer about 8 hours or overnight.
- Before serving, take out of the freezer about 45 minutes. For each serving, mix 1/2 cup lemon-lime soda with 1/2 cup slush mixture then stir well.

Nutrition Information

- Calories: 151 calories
- Cholesterol: 0 cholesterol
- Protein: 1g protein.
- Total Fat: 0 fat (0 saturated fat)
- Sodium: 22mg sodium
- Fiber: 1g fiber)
- Total Carbohydrate: 39g carbohydrate (35g sugars

286. Sherbet Punch

Serving: 4-1/2 quarts. | Prep: 10mins | Cook: 0mins | Ready in:

Ingredients

- 1/2 gallon lime or raspberry sherbet, softened
- 1 liter ginger ale
- 2 cups lemon-lime soda
- 2 cups grapefruit or citrus soda

Direction

- In a punch bowl, place sherbet right before serving. Pour in soda and ginger ale. Stir till sherbet almost dissolves.

Nutrition Information

- Calories: 132 calories
- Cholesterol: 4mg cholesterol
- Protein: 1g protein.
- Total Fat: 1g fat (1g saturated fat)
- Sodium: 39mg sodium
- Fiber: 0 fiber)
- Total Carbohydrate: 31g carbohydrate (27g sugars

287. Shrunken Apple Heads In Citrus Cider

Serving: about 1 gallon. | Prep: 35mins | Cook: 02hours00mins | Ready in:

Ingredients

- 1 cup lemon juice
- 1 tablespoon salt
- 4 large Granny Smith apples
- 16 whole cloves
- 1 gallon apple cider
- 1 can (12 ounces) frozen lemonade concentrate, thawed

Direction

- Mix salt and lemon juice in a bowl; set aside. Peel and slice every apple starting from the stem up to the apple's blossom end; remove core and seeds. Carefully carve a face on the round-side of every halved apple with a sharp knife. Submerge apples in the lemon juice mix for a minute; place on paper towels to drain.
- In a shallow baking dish, place apple heads. Bake apples at 250 degrees F oven for two hours or until they start to shrink, dry, and the edges are lightly brown. Cool apples on a wire rack then form eyes by inserting cloves; refrigerate.
- Mix lemonade and cider together in a punch bowl. Let the shrunken apples float in cider. Serve.

Nutrition Information

- Calories: 174 calories
- Sodium: 441mg sodium
- Fiber: 1g fiber)
- Total Carbohydrate: 44g carbohydrate (38g sugars
- Cholesterol: 0 cholesterol
- Protein: 0 protein.
- Total Fat: 0 fat (0 saturated fat)

288. Sidecar

Serving: 1 | Prep: 5mins | Cook: | Ready in:

Ingredients

- ice cubes
- 1/2 fluid ounce freshly squeezed lemon juice
- 1/2 fluid ounce Cointreau or triple sec
- 1 fluid ounce brandy
- 1 lemon wedge

Direction

- Add ice cubes to fill 3/4 of a cocktail shaker. Pour in brandy, Cointreau and lemon juice. Cover then shake vigorously for 30 seconds till it's frosty and cold on the outside of the shaker. In a martini glass, strain the drink and add a wedge of lemon for garnish.

289. Simple Citrus Punch

Serving: about 3 quarts. | Prep: 10mins | Cook: 0mins | Ready in:

Ingredients

- 1 can (12 ounces) frozen limeade concentrate, thawed
- 3/4 cup thawed lemonade concentrate
- 2 cups water

- 1/4 cup sugar, optional
- 2 liters ginger ale, chilled
- Ice cubes

Direction

- Combine lemonade and limeade concentrates in a large punch bowl. If desired, stir in sugar and water. Add in ginger ale and stir. Pour over ice and serve at once.

Nutrition Information

- Calories: 161 calories
- Protein: 0 protein.
- Total Fat: 0 fat (0 saturated fat)
- Sodium: 13mg sodium
- Fiber: 0 fiber)
- Total Carbohydrate: 42g carbohydrate (38g sugars
- Cholesterol: 0 cholesterol

290. Simple Lemon Berry Pitcher Punch

Serving: about 6 cups. | Prep: 10mins | Cook: 0mins | Ready in:

Ingredients

- 1/2 cup sweetened lemonade drink mix
- 4 cups cold water
- 2/3 cup cranberry juice, chilled
- 1-1/2 cups lemon-lime soda, chilled

Direction

- Mix together cranberry juice, water and drink mix in a pitcher, then stir in soda. Serve promptly.

Nutrition Information

- Calories: 106 calories
- Total Carbohydrate: 28g carbohydrate (19g sugars
- Cholesterol: 0 cholesterol
- Protein: 0 protein.
- Total Fat: 0 fat (0 saturated fat)
- Sodium: 11mg sodium
- Fiber: 0 fiber)

291. Six Vegetable Juice

Serving: 2 quarts. | Prep: 35mins | Cook: 30mins | Ready in:

Ingredients

- 5 pounds ripe tomatoes, peeled and chopped
- 1/2 cup water
- 1/4 cup chopped green pepper
- 1/4 cup chopped carrot
- 1/4 cup chopped celery
- 1/4 cup lemon juice
- 2 tablespoons chopped onion
- 1 tablespoon salt
- 1 to 1-1/2 small serrano peppers

Direction

- Combine the initial 8 ingredients in a Dutch oven. Discard seeds and stems from the serrano peppers if preferred. Place into the tomato mixture then boil. Lower heat then cover and let simmer till vegetables are tender, for 30 minutes. Let cool.
- Through a fine sieve or a food mill, press the mixture then store in a freezer or a fridge. Before serving stir or shake the juice well.

Nutrition Information

- Calories: 66 calories
- Sodium: 915mg sodium
- Fiber: 3g fiber)
- Total Carbohydrate: 15g carbohydrate (9g sugars

- Cholesterol: 0 cholesterol
- Protein: 3g protein.
- Total Fat: 1g fat (0 saturated fat)

292. So Healthy Smoothies

Serving: 4 servings. | Prep: 15mins | Cook: 0mins | Ready in:

Ingredients

- 1 cup fat-free milk
- 1/4 cup orange juice
- 2 tablespoons vanilla yogurt
- 1 tablespoon honey
- 1 small banana, sliced and frozen
- 2/3 cup frozen blueberries
- 1/2 cup chopped peeled mango, frozen
- 1-1/4 cups frozen unsweetened sliced peaches

Direction

- Mix all ingredients together in a blender then cover and blend until smooth. Transfer into cold glasses and serve promptly.

Nutrition Information

- Calories: 107 calories
- Sodium: 38mg sodium
- Fiber: 2g fiber)
- Total Carbohydrate: 24g carbohydrate (21g sugars
- Cholesterol: 2mg cholesterol
- Protein: 3g protein. Diabetic Exchanges: 1 fruit
- Total Fat: 1g fat (0 saturated fat)

293. Sour Mix

Serving: 3-2/3 cups. | Prep: 5mins | Cook: 10mins | Ready in:

Ingredients

- 2 cups sugar
- 1 cup water
- 3/4 cup lemon juice
- 3/4 cup lime juice

Direction

- Combine water and sugar in a small saucepan. Let boil over medium heat. Lower heat and simmer for 3-5 minutes, uncovered and stir occasionally to dissolve the sugar. Take away from the heat and let cool to room temperature.
- Pour into a container with a tight-fitting lid. Pour in lime juices and lemon. Refrigerate for up to 2 weeks.

Nutrition Information

- Calories: 28 calories
- Protein: 0 protein.
- Total Fat: 0 fat (0 saturated fat)
- Sodium: 0 sodium
- Fiber: 0 fiber)
- Total Carbohydrate: 7g carbohydrate (7g sugars
- Cholesterol: 0 cholesterol

294. Sparkling Citrus Quencher

Serving: 8 servings (2-1/2 quarts). | Prep: 5mins | Cook: 0mins | Ready in:

Ingredients

- 2 liters lemon-lime soda, chilled
- 3/4 cup limeade concentrate
- 1/2 cup orange juice

Direction

- Combine all of the ingredients in a large pitcher. Pour over ice to serve.

Nutrition Information

- Calories: 162 calories
- Total Carbohydrate: 42g carbohydrate (39g sugars
- Cholesterol: 0 cholesterol
- Protein: 0 protein.
- Total Fat: 0 fat (0 saturated fat)
- Sodium: 29mg sodium
- Fiber: 0 fiber)

295. Sparkling Fruit Punch

Serving: 2 quarts. | Prep: 5mins | Cook: 0mins | Ready in:

Ingredients

- 4 cups cold water
- 1 can (6 ounces) frozen orange juice concentrate, thawed
- 3/4 cup thawed lemonade concentrate
- 3/4 cup thawed grape juice concentrate
- 2 cups ginger ale, chilled
- Crushed ice

Direction

- Combine concentrates and water in a large bowl. Add in ginger ale and stir. Pour over ice to serve at once.

Nutrition Information

- Calories: 152 calories
- Sodium: 8mg sodium
- Fiber: 0 fiber)
- Total Carbohydrate: 38g carbohydrate (25g sugars
- Cholesterol: 0 cholesterol
- Protein: 1g protein.
- Total Fat: 0 fat (0 saturated fat)

296. Sparkling Peach Bellinis

Serving: 12 servings. | Prep: 10mins | Cook: 25mins | Ready in:

Ingredients

- 3 medium peaches, halved
- 1 tablespoon honey
- 1 can (11.3 ounces) peach nectar, chilled
- 2 bottles (750 milliliters each) champagne or sparkling grape juice, chilled

Direction

- Use a large piece of heavy-duty foil (about 18x12-in.) to line a baking sheet. Place peach halves on foil with the cut side facing up then drizzle over with honey. Fold over peaches and seal the foil.
- Bake for 25-30 minutes at 375° till tender. Let cool completely then remove and throw away peels. Process peaches in a food processor till smooth.
- In a pitcher, place peach puree then stir in 1 bottle of champagne and nectar till combined. Transfer into 12 wine glasses or champagne flutes then pour the leftover champagne on top. Serve at once.

Nutrition Information

- Calories: 74 calories
- Total Fat: 0 fat (0 saturated fat)
- Sodium: 2mg sodium
- Fiber: 1g fiber)
- Total Carbohydrate: 9g carbohydrate (7g sugars
- Cholesterol: 0 cholesterol
- Protein: 0 protein.

297. Sparkling Pom Berry Splash

Serving: 1 serving. | Prep: 5mins | Cook: 0mins | Ready in:

Ingredients

- 2 ounces pomegranate blueberry juice, chilled
- 1 teaspoon lime juice
- 1/3 cup sparkling moscato wine, chilled

Direction

- In a Champagne flute, pour lime juices and pomegranate blueberry. Add wine on top.

Nutrition Information

- Calories: 92 calories
- Protein: 0 protein.
- Total Fat: 0 fat (0 saturated fat)
- Sodium: 11mg sodium
- Fiber: 0 fiber)
- Total Carbohydrate: 10g carbohydrate (9g sugars
- Cholesterol: 0 cholesterol

298. Sparkling Punch

Serving: 20 | Prep: 10mins | Cook: | Ready in:

Ingredients

- 2 lemons
- 3 large oranges
- 1 (6 ounce) can frozen lemonade concentrate
- 1 liter club soda
- 2 (750 milliliter) bottles sparkling apple cider
- 1 tablespoon white sugar
- 2 trays ice cubes

Direction

- In a large punch bowl, place thinly sliced oranges and lemons. Add in thawed lemonade. Pour in sparkling apple cider and club soda; stir gently. Add sugar to suit your taste and place in ice.

Nutrition Information

- Calories: 73 calories;
- Total Fat: 0.1
- Sodium: 11
- Total Carbohydrate: 18.9
- Cholesterol: 0
- Protein: 0.4

299. Spiced Cider Punch

Serving: 12 servings (about 3-1/4 quarts). | Prep: 5mins | Cook: 5mins | Ready in:

Ingredients

- 1 cup sugar
- 1 teaspoon ground cinnamon
- 1 teaspoon ground allspice
- 1 bottle (64 ounces) apple cider or juice, divided
- 1 can (12 ounces) frozen orange juice concentrate
- 1 liter ginger ale, chilled
- Orange slices, optional

Direction

- On medium heat, cook and stir a cup of cider, spices, and sugar in a pit until the sugar dissolves. Take off heat. Mix in juice concentrate until dissolved.
- Move to a big pitcher and mix in the remaining cider. Place in the refrigerator while covered until chilled.
- Transfer the cider mixture on a punch bowl; mix in ginger ale. Add orange slices on top if desired. Serve.

Nutrition Information

- Calories: 217 calories
- Protein: 1g protein.
- Total Fat: 0 fat (0 saturated fat)
- Sodium: 25mg sodium
- Fiber: 0 fiber)
- Total Carbohydrate: 55g carbohydrate (50g sugars
- Cholesterol: 0 cholesterol

300. Spiced Green Tea

Serving: 12 servings (1 cup each). | Prep: 15mins | Cook: 10mins | Ready in:

Ingredients

- 5 cups water
- 5 individual green tea bags
- 1/2 cup sugar
- 1/4 teaspoon pumpkin pie spice
- 5 cups unsweetened apple juice
- 2 cups cranberry juice
- 1/3 cup lemon juice

Direction

- Bring water in a Dutch oven to a boil then take away from heat. Put in tea bags then soak about 6 to 8 minutes with a cover, depending on your taste.
- Get rid of tea bags then whisk in pie spice and sugar until sugar has dissolved. Whisk in the leftover ingredients. Chill and serve cold over ice or serve warm.

Nutrition Information

- Calories: 102 calories
- Sodium: 4mg sodium
- Fiber: 0 fiber)
- Total Carbohydrate: 26g carbohydrate (25g sugars
- Cholesterol: 0 cholesterol
- Protein: 0 protein.
- Total Fat: 0 fat (0 saturated fat)

301. Spiced Iced Tea

Serving: 2-4 servings. | Prep: 25mins | Cook: 0mins | Ready in:

Ingredients

- 4 cups boiling water
- 4 individual tea bags
- 1 cinnamon sticks (3 inches)
- 4 whole cloves
- Sugar substitute equivalent to 4 teaspoons sugar
- Ice cubes, fresh mint and lemon slices

Direction

- In a heat-proof pitcher, add boiling water then place in sugar substitute, cloves, cinnamon and tea bags. Let the tea steep for 15 minutes.
- Remove cloves, cinnamon and tea bags. Pour tea in glasses over ice. Add lemon and mint for garnish.

Nutrition Information

- Calories: 3 calories
- Sodium: 0 sodium
- Fiber: 0 fiber)
- Total Carbohydrate: 1g carbohydrate (0 sugars
- Cholesterol: 0 cholesterol
- Protein: 0 protein.
- Total Fat: 0 fat (0 saturated fat)

302. Spiced Pineapple Cooler

Serving: 13 servings (3/4 cup each). | Prep: 10mins | Cook: 20mins | Ready in:

Ingredients

- 1-1/2 cups water
- 2/3 cup sugar
- 4 cinnamon sticks (3 inches)
- 12 whole cloves
- 1 can (46 ounces) unsweetened pineapple juice
- 1-1/2 cups orange juice
- 1/2 cup lemon juice
- 1 can (12 ounces) ginger ale, chilled
- Ice cubes
- Additional cinnamon sticks, optional

Direction

- Boil cloves, cinnamon, sugar and water in a small saucepan. Lower heat then cover and let simmer for 15 minutes. Strain the drink then let cool to room temperature.
- Transfer into a large pitcher. Pour in juices and stir. Store in the fridge to chill. Add in ginger ale and stir right before serving. Pour over ice to serve. Place in additional cinnamon sticks for garnish if preferred.

Nutrition Information

- Calories: 119 calories
- Fiber: 0 fiber)
- Total Carbohydrate: 29g carbohydrate (25g sugars
- Cholesterol: 0 cholesterol
- Protein: 1g protein.
- Total Fat: 0 fat (0 saturated fat)
- Sodium: 4mg sodium

---

303. Spicy Homemade Tomato Juice

Serving: 15 servings (1 cup each). | Prep: 45mins | Cook: 20mins | Ready in:

Ingredients

- 12 pounds tomatoes
- 9 dried ancho chilies
- 3 medium onions, chopped
- 1 celery rib, chopped
- 1/4 cup chopped seeded jalapeno pepper
- 1/2 cup sugar
- 1 tablespoon Worcestershire sauce
- 2 teaspoons salt
- 1/4 teaspoon pepper

Direction

- Add water to fill 2/3 of a Dutch oven then boil. On the bottom of each tomato, make an X. One at a time, use a slotted spoon to place tomatoes in boiling water for 30-60 seconds. Discard the tomatoes and immediately transfer into the ice water. Remove peel, chop and put the tomatoes in a stockpot.
- Add jalapenos, celery, onions and chilies then boil. Lower heat and let simmer for 20-25 minutes, uncovered, till vegetables are tender. Let cool slightly. Process batches of juice in a food processor till blended. Strain and remove pulp and seeds. Transfer the puree in a Dutch oven.
- Add in the leftover ingredients, stir and heat through. Allow to cool. For serving, store in the fridge to chill or place into storage containers. Store in the freezer for up to 3 months or keep in the fridge for up to 3 days.

Nutrition Information

- Calories: 134 calories
- Protein: 5g protein. Diabetic Exchanges: 2 starch.
- Total Fat: 2g fat (0 saturated fat)
- Sodium: 351mg sodium
- Fiber: 7g fiber)
- Total Carbohydrate: 29g carbohydrate (18g sugars
- Cholesterol: 0 cholesterol

304. Spring Strawberry Sangria

Serving: 10 servings (about 2 quarts). | Prep: 10mins | Cook: 0mins | Ready in:

Ingredients

- 4 cups dry white wine, chilled
- 1/2 pound fresh strawberries, hulled and sliced
- 1/4 cup sugar
- 2 cups club soda, chilled
- 2 cups champagne

Direction

- Combine sugar, strawberries and wine in a pitcher. Store for at least 1 hour in the fridge.
- Pour in champagne and club soda then stir right before serving.

Nutrition Information

- Calories: 136 calories
- Total Carbohydrate: 10g carbohydrate (7g sugars
- Cholesterol: 0 cholesterol
- Protein: 0 protein.
- Total Fat: 0 fat (0 saturated fat)
- Sodium: 15mg sodium
- Fiber: 0 fiber)

305. Starry Fruit Punch

Serving: 4 quarts. | Prep: 10mins | Cook: 0mins | Ready in:

Ingredients

- 2 cups sugar
- 2 packages (.23 ounces each) unsweetened lime soft drink mix
- 6 cups water
- PUNCH:
- 1-1/2 cups sugar
- 1 package (6 ounces) raspberry gelatin
- 2 cups boiling water
- 6-1/2 cups cold water
- 6 ounces limeade concentrate
- 6 ounces lemonade concentrate
- 1 can (46 ounces) pineapple juice, chilled
- 2 liters ginger ale, chilled

Direction

- Dissolve drink mix and sugar in water in a bowl. Transfer to a 6-cup mold or 12 of 1/2-cup star-shaped mold. Leave in the freezer overnight.
- Dissolve gelatin and sugar in boiling water in a large bowl. Mix in concentrates and cold water. Allow to chill.
- Pour into a punch bowl just prior to serving; mix in ginger ale and pineapple juice. Put in 1 large mold or 3 small ice molds. If necessary, replenish small ice molds.

Nutrition Information

- Calories:
- Sodium:
- Fiber:
- Total Carbohydrate:
- Cholesterol:
- Protein:
- Total Fat:

306. Strawberry Banana Yogurt Shakes

Serving: 4 cups. | Prep: 10mins | Cook: 0mins | Ready in:

Ingredients

- 2 cups unsweetened frozen strawberries
- 1 medium banana
- 1 cup (8 ounces) plain yogurt
- 1 cup milk
- 1/2 cup orange juice

- 2 tablespoons honey
- 1 teaspoon vanilla extract

Direction

- Mix all the ingredients in a blender; cover and process the ingredients until smooth. Pour the blended drink into the thermos or other insulated containers. Keep the drink cool. Just shake it before serving.

Nutrition Information

- Calories: 174 calories
- Sodium: 58mg sodium
- Fiber: 2g fiber)
- Total Carbohydrate: 31g carbohydrate (27g sugars
- Cholesterol: 16mg cholesterol
- Protein: 5g protein.
- Total Fat: 4g fat (3g saturated fat)

307. Strawberry Banana Yogurt Smoothie

Serving: 2 servings. | Prep: 5mins | Cook: 0mins | Ready in:

Ingredients

- 1/2 cup 2% milk
- 1/3 cup strawberry yogurt
- 1/3 cup frozen unsweetened strawberries
- 1/2 medium firm banana, chopped
- 4 ice cubes
- 8 teaspoons sugar

Direction

- Mix all of ingredients in a blender then cover and blend until smooth, about 30-45 seconds. Stir if needed. Transfer into cold glasses and serve promptly.

Nutrition Information

- Calories: 170 calories
- Total Carbohydrate: 36g carbohydrate (33g sugars
- Cholesterol: 7mg cholesterol
- Protein: 4g protein.
- Total Fat: 2g fat (1g saturated fat)
- Sodium: 53mg sodium
- Fiber: 1g fiber)

308. Strawberry Breakfast Shakes

Serving: 4 servings. | Prep: 5mins | Cook: 0mins | Ready in:

Ingredients

- 1-1/4 cups plain yogurt
- 1 package (10 ounces) frozen sweetened sliced strawberries
- 2/3 cup milk
- 2/3 cup crushed ice
- 1 tablespoon honey
- 4 whole strawberries

Direction

- Mix the first five ingredients in a blender. Cover the blender and process it until thick and smooth. Pour the mixture into the chilled glasses. Garnish the drink with whole strawberries and serve.

Nutrition Information

- Calories: 159 calories
- Protein: 4g protein.
- Total Fat: 4g fat (2g saturated fat)
- Sodium: 58mg sodium
- Fiber: 2g fiber)
- Total Carbohydrate: 29g carbohydrate (27g sugars

- Cholesterol: 15mg cholesterol

309. Strawberry Cilantro Lemonade

Serving: 15 servings (1 cup each). | Prep: 25mins | Cook: 0mins | Ready in:

Ingredients

- 1-1/2 cups lemon juice
- 1-3/4 cups sugar
- 6 cups fresh or frozen strawberries, thawed
- 3/4 cup fresh cilantro leaves
- 3 quarts cold water
- Ice cubes

Direction

- In a blender, put in cilantro, strawberries, sugar and lemon juice. Cover and blend until combined. Strain and get rid of pulp.
- Mix equal amounts of water and strawberries mixture in 2 pitchers. Serve over ice.

Nutrition Information

- Calories: 115 calories
- Protein: 0 protein. Diabetic Exchanges: 1-1/2 starch
- Total Fat: 0 fat (0 saturated fat)
- Sodium: 1mg sodium
- Fiber: 1g fiber)
- Total Carbohydrate: 30g carbohydrate (27g sugars
- Cholesterol: 0 cholesterol

310. Strawberry Citrus Slushies

Serving: 5 servings. | Prep: 10mins | Cook: 0mins | Ready in:

Ingredients

- STRAWBERRY PUREE:
- 1/2 cup frozen unsweetened sliced strawberries, thawed
- 2 tablespoons confectioners' sugar
- 2 tablespoons water
- CITRUS SLUSH:
- 3/4 cup sugar
- 3/4 cup water
- 3/4 cup lemon juice
- 2/3 cup orange juice
- 4-1/2 cups ice cubes

Direction

- In a blender, add water, confectioners' sugar and strawberries. Cover and blend until combined then turn to a small bowl. Cover and refrigerate until serving.
- Bring water and sugar in a small saucepan to a boil. Cook and stir until sugar has dissolved. Take away from heat then allow to cool to room temperature.
- Right before serving, in a blender, add sugar syrup, ice cubes, orange juice and lemon juice. Cover and blend until gets a slushy consistency. Split among 4 cold glasses with strawberry puree. Place citrus slush on top and serve promptly.

Nutrition Information

- Calories: 157 calories
- Protein: 0 protein.
- Total Fat: 0 fat (0 saturated fat)
- Sodium: 3mg sodium
- Fiber: 0 fiber)
- Total Carbohydrate: 41g carbohydrate (37g sugars
- Cholesterol: 0 cholesterol

311. Strawberry Cooler

Serving: Serves 1 | Prep: | Cook: | Ready in:

Ingredients

- 1/2 cup sliced, hulled strawberries
- 1 pony (1 ounce) whiskey
- 1 pony (1 ounce) Southern Comfort
- 1 pony (1 ounce) Grand Marnier
- 1 pony (1 ounce) lemon juice
- 1 tablespoon superfine granulated sugar, or to taste
- 1 cup cracked ice
- Garnish: slice of orange

Direction

- Blend sugar (if preferred), lemon juice, Southern Comfort, whiskey and strawberries in a blender for 10 seconds. Place in cracked ice then blend for 15 seconds. Transfer into a chilled 12-ounce glass. Add orange slice for garnish.

Nutrition Information

- Calories: 383
- Saturated Fat: 0 g(0%)
- Sodium: 16 mg(1%)
- Fiber: 2 g(7%)
- Total Carbohydrate: 39 g(13%)
- Protein: 1 g(2%)
- Total Fat: 1 g(1%)

312. Strawberry Flax Smoothies

Serving: 2 servings. | Prep: 10mins | Cook: 0mins | Ready in:

Ingredients

- 1 cup refrigerated strawberry breeze juice blend
- 2 cups ice cubes
- 1-1/2 cups frozen unsweetened strawberries
- 1/2 medium banana
- 2 tablespoons ground flaxseed

Direction

- Mix whole ingredients in a blender, then cover and blend until smooth. Transfer into cold glasses and serve promptly.

Nutrition Information

- Calories: 167 calories
- Cholesterol: 0 cholesterol
- Protein: 2g protein.
- Total Fat: 4g fat (1g saturated fat)
- Sodium: 9mg sodium
- Fiber: 5g fiber)
- Total Carbohydrate: 36g carbohydrate (29g sugars

313. Strawberry Lemonade Slush

Serving: 4 servings. | Prep: 5mins | Cook: 0mins | Ready in:

Ingredients

- 3/4 cup water
- 3/4 cup thawed pink lemonade concentrate
- 1 package (10 ounces) frozen sweetened sliced strawberries, thawed
- 3/4 cup ice cubes
- 1 cup club soda

Direction

- Combine ice cubes, lemonade concentrate, strawberries, and water in a blender. Cover the blender and blend the mixture until combined.

- Pour the mixture into the freezer container. Cover and freeze it for at least 12 hours or it can be up to 3 months.
- Before serving it, allow it to stand at room temperature for 1 hour. Mix in club soda. Pour the mixture into the chilled glasses. Serve.

Nutrition Information

- Calories: 167 calories
- Fiber: 2g fiber)
- Total Carbohydrate: 44g carbohydrate (40g sugars
- Cholesterol: 0 cholesterol
- Protein: 1g protein.
- Total Fat: 0 fat (0 saturated fat)
- Sodium: 17mg sodium

314. Strawberry Lime Smoothies

Serving: 3 servings. | Prep: 5mins | Cook: 0mins | Ready in:

Ingredients

- 1 cup (8 ounces) strawberry yogurt
- 1/2 cup 2% milk
- 2 to 4 tablespoons lime juice
- 2 tablespoons honey
- 1/4 teaspoon ground cinnamon
- 2 cups fresh strawberries, hulled

Direction

- In a blender, process all of the ingredients, covered till smooth.

Nutrition Information

- Calories: 172 calories
- Fiber: 2g fiber)
- Total Carbohydrate: 36g carbohydrate (32g sugars
- Cholesterol: 7mg cholesterol
- Protein: 5g protein.
- Total Fat: 2g fat (1g saturated fat)
- Sodium: 61mg sodium

315. Strawberry Mango Smoothies For 2

Serving: 2 servings. | Prep: 10mins | Cook: 0mins | Ready in:

Ingredients

- 1/2 cup fat-free milk
- 1/4 cup vanilla yogurt
- 3/4 cup halved fresh strawberries
- 1/2 medium mango, peeled and chopped
- 2 to 3 ice cubes
- Sugar substitute equivalent to 1-1/2 teaspoons sugar

Direction

- Mix all ingredients in a blender, then cover and blend until smooth for 20 to 30 seconds. Stir if needed, then transfer into cold glasses and serve promptly.

Nutrition Information

- Calories: 100 calories
- Fiber: 2g fiber)
- Total Carbohydrate: 21g carbohydrate (18g sugars
- Cholesterol: 3mg cholesterol
- Protein: 4g protein. Diabetic Exchanges: 1 fruit
- Total Fat: 1g fat (0 saturated fat)
- Sodium: 47mg sodium

316. Strawberry Melon Fizz

Serving: 10 servings. | Prep: 30mins | Cook: 0mins | Ready in:

Ingredients

- 2 cups sugar
- 1 cup water
- 5 fresh mint sprigs
- 1 quart fresh strawberries, halved
- 2 cups cubed honeydew
- 1-3/4 cups cubed cantaloupe
- Ginger ale or sparkling white grape juice

Direction

- Combine mint, water and sugar in a large saucepan then boil. Let boil while stirring till soft-ball stage and it reads 240° on a candy thermometer. Take away from the heat and let cool. Remove the mint.
- Combine melon and strawberries. Right before serving, add fruit to fill tall glasses and sprinkle 1 tbsp. of syrup. Pour ginger ale into each.

Nutrition Information

- Calories: 194 calories
- Cholesterol: 0 cholesterol
- Protein: 1g protein.
- Total Fat: 0 fat (0 saturated fat)
- Sodium: 7mg sodium
- Fiber: 2g fiber)
- Total Carbohydrate: 49g carbohydrate (46g sugars

317. Strawberry Party Punch

Serving: 13 servings (3/4 cup each). | Prep: 15mins | Cook: 0mins | Ready in:

Ingredients

- 6 cups fresh or frozen unsweetened strawberries, thawed
- 3/4 cup thawed limeade concentrate
- 1 can (6 ounces) unsweetened pineapple juice
- 4 cups chilled lemon-lime soda
- Ice cubes, optional

Direction

- In a food processor, place strawberries and process, covered, till smooth. Add pineapple juice and limeade concentrate, stir. Let chill till serving.
- Pour in a punch bowl. Add soda and stir just before serving. Pour over ice to serve if preferred.

Nutrition Information

- Calories: 101 calories
- Cholesterol: 0 cholesterol
- Protein: 1g protein.
- Total Fat: 0 fat (0 saturated fat)
- Sodium: 9mg sodium
- Fiber: 1g fiber)
- Total Carbohydrate: 25g carbohydrate (23g sugars

318. Strawberry Peach Banana Smoothie

Serving: 2-1/2 cups. | Prep: 5mins | Cook: 0mins | Ready in:

Ingredients

- 1-1/4 cups milk
- 1 cup frozen unsweetened strawberries
- 1/2 cup frozen unsweetened sliced peaches
- 1 small ripe banana, halved
- 3 tablespoons sugar

Direction

- In a blender, add all ingredients, then cover and blend until smooth. Transfer into cold glasses and serve promptly.

Nutrition Information

- Calories: 250 calories
- Sodium: 63mg sodium
- Fiber: 3g fiber)
- Total Carbohydrate: 47g carbohydrate (39g sugars
- Cholesterol: 15mg cholesterol
- Protein: 6g protein.
- Total Fat: 5g fat (3g saturated fat)

319. Strawberry Pineapple Punch

Serving: 22 servings. | Prep: 10mins | Cook: 0mins | Ready in:

Ingredients

- 1 package (20 ounces) frozen unsweetened strawberries, thawed
- 1 can (46 ounces) unsweetened pineapple juice
- 2-1/2 cups orange juice
- 1/2 cup lemon juice
- 2 liters diet lemon-lime soda

Direction

- In a blender, place the strawberries then cover and puree till smooth. Place into a large freezer container then pour in juices. Cover and let freeze. 2-3 hours before serving, take the mixture out of the freezer. Use a potato masher or a wooden spoon to break up the mixture right before serving. Add in soda and stir.

Nutrition Information

- Calories: 59 calories
- Protein: 1g protein. Diabetic Exchanges: 1 fruit.
- Total Fat: 0 fat (0 saturated fat)
- Sodium: 14mg sodium
- Fiber: 0 fiber)
- Total Carbohydrate: 15g carbohydrate (0 sugars
- Cholesterol: 0 cholesterol

320. Strawberry Shakes

Serving: Makes 2 (16-oz) shakes | Prep: 10mins | Cook: 10mins | Ready in:

Ingredients

- 3 cups premium vanilla ice cream
- 2 cups sliced strawberries (19 oz whole)
- 1 cup whole milk

Direction

- Blend all the ingredients in a blender until smooth.

Nutrition Information

- Calories: 537
- Saturated Fat: 16 g(79%)
- Sodium: 213 mg(9%)
- Fiber: 5 g(19%)
- Total Carbohydrate: 65 g(22%)
- Cholesterol: 99 mg(33%)
- Protein: 12 g(24%)
- Total Fat: 26 g(40%)

321. Strawberry Smoothie

Serving: 2 | Prep: | Cook: 5mins | Ready in:

Ingredients

- 1 cup fresh strawberries, rinsed and hulled, or frozen strawberries, partially thawed
- 1 cup buttermilk
- ½ cup frozen cranberry juice concentrate
- 2 ice cubes, crushed
- 1 teaspoon sugar, (optional)

Direction

- In a blender, mix together crushed ice, cranberry juice concentrate, buttermilk and strawberries. Cover and process until frothy and smooth. Add in sugar to sweeten if wanted. Serve promptly.

Nutrition Information

- Calories: 205 calories;
- Total Fat: 1
- Saturated Fat: 1
- Fiber: 2
- Cholesterol: 4
- Sugar: 39
- Sodium: 179
- Total Carbohydrate: 18
- Protein: 4

322. Strawberry Yogurt Smoothies

Serving: 4 servings. | Prep: 10mins | Cook: 0mins | Ready in:

Ingredients

- 3 cups sliced unsweetened strawberries
- 1 cup (8 ounces) fat-free vanilla yogurt
- 1 cup fat-free milk
- 2 tablespoons nonfat dry milk powder
- 2 tablespoons sugar
- 2 tablespoons reduced-sugar strawberry fruit spread

Direction

- Mix all ingredients in a food processor or a blender. Cover and blend until smooth then transfer into cold glasses and serve promptly.

Nutrition Information

- Calories: 153 calories
- Cholesterol: 3mg cholesterol
- Protein: 6g protein. Diabetic Exchanges: 1 fruit
- Total Fat: 0 fat (0 saturated fat)
- Sodium: 79mg sodium
- Fiber: 3g fiber)
- Total Carbohydrate: 32g carbohydrate (0 sugars

323. Strawberry Carrot Smoothies

Serving: 5 servings. | Prep: 5mins | Cook: 0mins | Ready in:

Ingredients

- 2 cups (16 ounces) reduced-fat plain Greek yogurt
- 1 cup carrot juice
- 1 cup orange juice
- 1 cup frozen pineapple chunks
- 1 cup frozen unsweetened sliced strawberries

Direction

- In a blender, add all ingredients. Cover and blend until smooth.

Nutrition Information

- Calories: 141 calories
- Fiber: 1g fiber)
- Total Carbohydrate: 20g carbohydrate (15g sugars
- Cholesterol: 5mg cholesterol
- Protein: 10g protein. Diabetic Exchanges: 1 fruit

- Total Fat: 2g fat (1g saturated fat)
- Sodium: 79mg sodium

324. Strawberry Peach Milk Shakes

Serving: 4 servings. | Prep: 15mins | Cook: 0mins | Ready in:

Ingredients

- 1/4 cup milk
- 3 tablespoons sugar
- 2 cups halved fresh strawberries
- 1-3/4 cups sliced peeled peaches (about 3 medium) or frozen unsweetened sliced peaches, thawed
- 2 cups vanilla ice cream

Direction

- In a blender, process the strawberries, milk, peaches, and sugar until the fruits are pureed. Add the ice cream and process the mixture again until well-blended. Serve it immediately.

Nutrition Information

- Calories: 230 calories
- Total Carbohydrate: 38g carbohydrate (31g sugars
- Cholesterol: 31mg cholesterol
- Protein: 4g protein.
- Total Fat: 8g fat (5g saturated fat)
- Sodium: 60mg sodium
- Fiber: 3g fiber)

325. Sugar Free Holiday Nog

Serving: 8 servings. | Prep: 10mins | Cook: 0mins | Ready in:

Ingredients

- 1 package (1 ounce) sugar-free instant vanilla pudding mix
- 7 cups fat-free milk, divided
- 1 to 2 teaspoons vanilla extract or rum extract
- 2 to 4 packets sugar substitute
- 1 cup fat-free evaporated milk

Direction

- In a bowl, following the pudding directions, mix 2 cups of milk, sugar substitute, pudding mix and vanilla.
- Prepare a half-gallon container with a tight-fitting lid, pour in the mixture. Pour 3 cups of milk and shake well. Pour evaporated milk, shake. Pour remaining milk; shake well. Let it chill.

Nutrition Information

- Calories: 107 calories
- Protein: 10g protein. Diabetic Exchanges: 1 fat-free milk
- Total Fat: 1g fat (0 saturated fat)
- Sodium: 187mg sodium
- Fiber: 0 fiber)
- Total Carbohydrate: 15g carbohydrate (0 sugars
- Cholesterol: 1mg cholesterol

326. Summertime Fruit Tea

Serving: 3-1/2 quarts. | Prep: 15mins | Cook: 0mins | Ready in:

Ingredients

- 12 cups water, divided
- 1-1/2 cups sugar
- 9 individual tea bags
- 1 can (12 ounces) frozen lemonade concentrate, thawed

- 1 can (12 ounces) frozen pineapple-orange juice concentrate, thawed

Direction

- Boil 4 cups of water in a Dutch oven. Add in sugar then stir to dissolve. Take away from the heat then place in tea bags. Let steep for 5-8 minutes. Remove the tea bags. Add in the leftover water and juice concentrates then stir. Pour over ice then serve.

Nutrition Information

- Calories: 173 calories
- Protein: 0 protein.
- Total Fat: 0 fat (0 saturated fat)
- Sodium: 15mg sodium
- Fiber: 0 fiber)
- Total Carbohydrate: 44g carbohydrate (41g sugars
- Cholesterol: 0 cholesterol

327. Summertime Tea

Serving: 18 servings (3/4 cup each). | Prep: 15mins | Cook: 0mins | Ready in:

Ingredients

- 14 cups water, divided
- 6 individual black tea bags
- 1-1/2 cups sugar
- 3/4 cup thawed orange juice concentrate
- 3/4 cup thawed lemonade concentrate
- 1 cup tequila, optional
- Fresh mint leaves and lemon or lime slices, optional

Direction

- Bring 4 cups water in a big saucepan to a boil. Take away from heat and put in tea bags. Cover and soak for 3 to 5 minutes. Get rid of the tea bags.
- Stir in the leftover water, concentrates and sugar. Add in tequila if you want then place in the fridge to chill until cold. Decorate with lemon and mint if you want.

Nutrition Information

- Calories: 0
- Total Carbohydrate: 1mg sodium
- Cholesterol: 0 fat (0 saturated fat)
- Protein: 0 fiber)
- Total Fat: mint and lemon): 102 calories
- Sodium: 0 cholesterol
- Fiber: 26g carbohydrate (26g sugars

328. Sun Kissed Smoothies

Serving: 3 servings. | Prep: 10mins | Cook: 0mins | Ready in:

Ingredients

- 3/4 cup ruby red grapefruit juice
- 1 medium ripe banana, cut into chunks and frozen
- 1/2 cup cubed fresh pineapple
- 1/2 cup frozen unsweetened peach slices
- 4 ice cubes
- 1 tablespoon sugar

Direction

- Mix all ingredients in a blender, then cover and blend until smooth for 30-45 seconds. Transfer into cold glasses and serve promptly.

Nutrition Information

- Calories: 100 calories
- Sodium: 2mg sodium
- Fiber: 2g fiber)
- Total Carbohydrate: 25g carbohydrate (22g sugars
- Cholesterol: 0 cholesterol

- Protein: 1g protein. Diabetic Exchanges: 1 fruit
- Total Fat: 0 fat (0 saturated fat)

329. Sunny Orange Lemonade

Serving: 6 | Prep: 5mins | Cook: 15mins | Ready in:

Ingredients

- 4 1/4 cups water, divided
- 1 cup sugar
- 3/4 cup lemon juice
- 3/4 cup orange juice
- 2 teaspoons grated lemon peel
- 1 teaspoon grated orange peel
- ice cubes
- Lemon slices

Direction

- Add sugar and 1 1/4 cups water in a saucepan and bring to a boil. Lower heat. Simmer about 10 minutes and cool. Turn the mixture into a pitcher and put in lemon and orange peels and juices. Cover and chill in the fridge for minimum of an hour. Whisk in the leftover water. Serve over ice and if you want, decorate with lemon.

330. Sunny Slush

Serving: 3 quarts. | Prep: 10mins | Cook: 0mins | Ready in:

Ingredients

- 6 cups pineapple juice
- 4 pints lemon sherbet
- 24 ice cubes
- 1 teaspoon rum extract

Direction

- Mix together extract, ice, sherbet, and pineapple juice in a blender, working in batches. Cover and blend until smooth. Transfer into cold glasses and serve promptly.

Nutrition Information

- Calories: 210 calories
- Total Fat: 2g fat (1g saturated fat)
- Sodium: 48mg sodium
- Fiber: 4g fiber)
- Total Carbohydrate: 46g carbohydrate (36g sugars
- Cholesterol: 0 cholesterol
- Protein: 2g protein.

331. Sunrise Sipper

Serving: 1 serving. | Prep: 5mins | Cook: 0mins | Ready in:

Ingredients

- Ice cubes
- 2 tablespoons grenadine syrup
- 1-1/2 ounces vodka
- 1/2 cup orange juice

Direction

- Add ice to fill a tall glass. Pour in vodka and grenadine. Add orange juice over the top.

Nutrition Information

- Calories: 213 calories
- Sodium: 5mg sodium
- Fiber: 1g fiber)
- Total Carbohydrate: 28g carbohydrate (25g sugars
- Cholesterol: 0 cholesterol
- Protein: 1g protein.
- Total Fat: 0 fat (0 saturated fat)

332. Sunrise Slushies

Serving: 8 servings. | Prep: 10mins | Cook: 0mins | Ready in:

Ingredients

- 2 cups orange juice
- 1 cup reduced-calorie reduced-sugar cranberry juice
- 1 medium tart apple, chopped
- 1/2 cup cubed peeled mango
- 2 kiwifruit, peeled, sliced and quartered
- 2 cups halved fresh strawberries
- 8 to 10 ice cubes

Direction

- Put half of per ingredient into a blender. Cover and blend until smooth then transfer into cold glasses. Do the same process with the leftover ingredients and serve promptly.

Nutrition Information

- Calories: 73 calories
- Total Fat: 0 fat (0 saturated fat)
- Sodium: 2mg sodium
- Fiber: 2g fiber)
- Total Carbohydrate: 18g carbohydrate (14g sugars
- Cholesterol: 0 cholesterol
- Protein: 1g protein. Diabetic Exchanges: 1 fruit.

333. Super Mango Smoothies

Serving: 2 servings. | Prep: 10mins | Cook: 0mins | Ready in:

Ingredients

- 1-1/2 cups peach mango juice blend
- 1 cup frozen pineapple chunks
- 1 cup frozen mango chunks
- 2 tablespoons 2% cottage cheese
- 2 tablespoons ground flaxseed
- 1 tablespoon toasted wheat germ

Direction

- Mix all ingredients in a blender, then cover and blend until smooth, or for 1 minute. Transfer into cold glasses and serve promptly.

Nutrition Information

- Calories: 269 calories
- Sodium: 86mg sodium
- Fiber: 5g fiber)
- Total Carbohydrate: 56g carbohydrate (41g sugars
- Cholesterol: 2mg cholesterol
- Protein: 5g protein.
- Total Fat: 4g fat (0 saturated fat)

334. Sweet Citrus Iced Tea

Serving: 1 gallon. | Prep: 15mins | Cook: 0mins | Ready in:

Ingredients

- 14-1/2 cups water, divided
- 10 individual tea bags
- 1-1/2 cups sugar
- 2/3 cup lemon juice
- 1/4 cup thawed orange juice concentrate
- Ice cubes

Direction

- Boil 4 cups of water in a large saucepan. Take away from the heat. Place in tea bags and allow to stand for 10 minutes. Remove the tea bags.
- Transfer into a large container. Add in the leftover water, orange juice concentrate, lemon

juice and sugar then stir. Store in the fridge to chill. Pour over ice to serve.

Nutrition Information

- Calories: 82 calories
- Protein: 0 protein. Diabetic Exchanges: 1-1/2 fruit.
- Total Fat: 0 fat (0 saturated fat)
- Sodium: 0 sodium
- Fiber: 0 fiber)
- Total Carbohydrate: 21g carbohydrate (20g sugars
- Cholesterol: 0 cholesterol

335. Sweet Citrus Punch

Serving: 12 servings (about 3 quarts). | Prep: 5mins | Cook: 0mins |Ready in:

Ingredients

- 1 can (12 ounces) frozen orange juice concentrate, thawed
- 1 can (12 ounces) frozen lemonade concentrate, thawed
- 1 cup grenadine syrup
- 2 quarts ginger ale, chilled
- Ice ring or shaved ice, optional

Direction

- Combine ginger ale, grenadine and concentrates in a punch bowl right before serving. Place in shaved ice or an ice ring if preferred.

Nutrition Information

- Calories: 192 calories
- Sodium: 17mg sodium
- Fiber: 1g fiber)
- Total Carbohydrate: 48g carbohydrate (46g sugars

- Cholesterol: 0 cholesterol
- Protein: 1g protein.
- Total Fat: 0 fat (0 saturated fat)

336. Sweet Raspberry Tea

Serving: 15 servings. | Prep: 10mins | Cook: 15mins | Ready in:

Ingredients

- 4 quarts water, divided
- 10 individual tea bags
- 1 package (12 ounces) frozen unsweetened raspberries, thawed and undrained
- 1 cup sugar
- 3 tablespoons lime juice

Direction

- Boil 2 quarts of water in a saucepan; take away from the heat. Place in tea bags, cover and let steep for 5-8 minutes according to your taste. Remove the tea bags.
- In a large saucepan, boil the leftover water with sugar and raspberries then stir till sugar is dissolved. Lower heat, uncover and let simmer for 3 minutes. Press the mixture into a bowl through a fine-mesh strainer. Remove seeds and pulp.
- Combine lime juice, raspberry syrup and tea in a large pitcher. Store in the fridge till cold, covered.

Nutrition Information

- Calories: 63 calories
- Total Carbohydrate: 16g carbohydrate (15g sugars
- Cholesterol: 0 cholesterol
- Protein: 0 protein.
- Total Fat: 0 fat (0 saturated fat)
- Sodium: 0 sodium
- Fiber: 1g fiber)

- Protein: 0 protein.
- Total Fat: 0 fat (0 saturated fat)

337. Sweet Tea Concentrate

Serving: 20 servings (5 cups concentrate). | Prep: 20mins | Cook: 10mins | Ready in:

Ingredients

- 2 medium lemons
- 4 cups sugar
- 4 cups water
- 1-1/2 cups English breakfast tea leaves or 20 black tea bags
- 1/3 cup lemon juice
- EACH SERVING:
- 1 cup cold water
- Ice cubes

Direction

- Discard the lemons' peels and set fruit aside to use in other times.
- Combine water and sugar in a large saucepan. Boil over medium heat. Lower heat and simmer while stirring occasionally, uncovered, for 3-5 minutes till the sugar dissolves. Take away from the heat then place in lemon peels and tea leaves. Steep, covered, for 15 minutes. Strain the tea; remove lemon peels and tea leaves; mix in lemon juice. Let cool till room temperature.
- Place in a container with tight-fitting lid. Refrigerate for up to 2 weeks.
- For tea: Combine 1/4 cup of concentrate with water in a tall glass. Place in ice.

Nutrition Information

- Calories: 165 calories
- Sodium: 27mg sodium
- Fiber: 0 fiber)
- Total Carbohydrate: 43g carbohydrate (40g sugars
- Cholesterol: 0 cholesterol

338. Tangy Fruit Punch

Serving: 8 servings, 1 cup each | Prep: 5mins | Cook: | Ready in:

Ingredients

- 3 cups cold pineapple juice
- 1/4 cup fresh lemon juice
- 1/4 cup fresh lime juice
- 3/4 cup TANG Orange Flavor Drink Mix
- 1/4 cup KOOL-AID Tropical Punch Flavor Sugar-Sweetened Drink Mix
- 1 bottle (1 L) ginger ale, chilled

Direction

- In a punch bowl, place the combined drink mixes and add juices. Stir to dissolve completely.
- Store in the fridge till chilled, for several hours.
- Add in ginger ale and stir right before pouring over ice to serve.

Nutrition Information

- Calories: 190
- Sugar: 47 g
- Total Carbohydrate: 49 g
- Cholesterol: 0 mg
- Protein: 0 g
- Total Fat: 0 g
- Fiber: 0 g
- Sodium: 40 mg
- Saturated Fat: 0 g

339. Tangy Party Punch

Serving: 8 quarts. | Prep: 10mins | Cook: 0mins | Ready in:

Ingredients

- 1 can (46 ounces) pineapple juice, chilled
- 1 can (46 ounces) orange juice, chilled
- 1 can (12 ounces) frozen limeade concentrate, thawed
- 1 can (12 ounces) frozen lemonade concentrate, thawed
- 3 liters ginger ale, chilled
- 1 pint each orange, lemon and lime sherbet

Direction

- Combine the initial 4 ingredients in a large punch bowl. Add in ginger ale and stir. Place in scoops of sherbet. Serve at once.

Nutrition Information

- Calories: 155 calories
- Protein: 1g protein.
- Total Fat: 1g fat (0 saturated fat)
- Sodium: 20mg sodium
- Fiber: 0 fiber)
- Total Carbohydrate: 38g carbohydrate (34g sugars
- Cholesterol: 2mg cholesterol

340. Tangy Strawberry Slush

Serving: 26 servings (3/4 cup each). | Prep: 10mins | Cook: 0mins | Ready in:

Ingredients

- 9 cups water, divided
- 3 cups sugar
- 4 individual tea bags
- 1 pint fresh strawberries, stems removed
- 1 cup cranberry juice
- 3/4 cup thawed orange juice concentrate
- 3/4 cup thawed lemonade concentrate
- 6-1/2 cups lemon-lime soda, chilled

Direction

- Bring sugar and 7 cups water in a big saucepan to a boil. Stir until sugar has dissolved. Take away from heat and allow to cool.
- At the same time, bring the leftover water in a small saucepan to a boil. Take away from heat then put tea bags in. Cover and let soak for 3 to 5 minutes. Get rid of tea bags and allow to cool. Turn tea and sugar mixtures to a 4-qt. freezer container.
- Mix together juice concentrates, cranberry juice and strawberries in a blender, then cover and blend until blended. Stir into the freezer container and let it cool. Cover and place in the freezer about 6 hours or overnight.
- To serve, mix in a glass with 1/4 cup soda and 1/2 cup strawberry mixture then serve promptly.

Nutrition Information

- Calories: 152 calories
- Cholesterol: 0 cholesterol
- Protein: 0 protein.
- Total Fat: 0 fat (0 saturated fat)
- Sodium: 8mg sodium
- Fiber: 0 fiber)
- Total Carbohydrate: 39g carbohydrate (38g sugars

341. Tequila Sunrise

Serving: 1 | Prep: 5mins | Cook: | Ready in:

Ingredients

- 1 (1.5 fluid ounce) jigger tequila
- 3/4 cup freshly squeezed orange juice

- ice cubes
- 1/2 (1.5 fluid ounce) jigger grenadine syrup
- 1 slice orange, for garnish
- 1 maraschino cherry for garnish

Direction

- Shake or stir orange juice and tequila together. Add ice cubes to fill a chilled 12-ounce glass. Place in the orange juice mixture. Pour the grenadine in gradually; be patient and let it settle to the glass's bottom. Add a maraschino cherry and a slice of orange as garnish.

342. Thick Peachy Milk Shakes

Serving: 4 servings. | Prep: 10mins | Cook: 0mins | Ready in:

Ingredients

- 3/4 cup cold 2% milk
- 1/4 cup peach nectar or orange juice
- 1 tablespoon honey
- 2 cups sliced peeled fresh or frozen peaches, thawed
- 3 cups vanilla ice cream

Direction

- Combine the peaches, milk, honey, and peach nectar in a blender. Cover it and process until smooth. Add the ice cream and process for 30 more seconds or until smooth. Pour the mixture into the chilled glasses and serve.

Nutrition Information

- Calories: 279 calories
- Total Fat: 12g fat (7g saturated fat)
- Sodium: 103mg sodium
- Fiber: 1g fiber)
- Total Carbohydrate: 40g carbohydrate (33g sugars

- Cholesterol: 47mg cholesterol
- Protein: 6g protein.

343. Thirst Quenching Limeade

Serving: 7 servings (1-3/4 quarts). | Prep: 10mins | Cook: 10mins | Ready in:

Ingredients

- 5-1/2 cups water, divided
- 1-1/4 cups sugar
- 3/4 cup lemon juice (about 4 lemons)
- 3/4 cup lime juice (about 4 limes)
- 1 teaspoon grated lemon zest
- 1 teaspoon grated lime zest
- Ice cubes

Direction

- Add in sugar and 1 1/2 cups water in a big saucepan then bring to a boil. Lower heat and simmer for about 10 minutes, without a cover. Let it cool to room temperature.
- Turn to a 2-qt. pitcher then stir in peels and juices. Cover and place it in the fridge to chill for minimum of 1 hour. Stir in leftover water and serve over ice.

Nutrition Information

- Calories: 152 calories
- Protein: 0 protein.
- Total Fat: 0 fat (0 saturated fat)
- Sodium: 1mg sodium
- Fiber: 0 fiber)
- Total Carbohydrate: 40g carbohydrate (37g sugars
- Cholesterol: 0 cholesterol

344. Three Fruit Slushies

Serving: 14 servings. | Prep: 15mins | Cook: 0mins | Ready in:

Ingredients

- 2 cups sugar
- 3 cups boiling water
- 1 can (12 ounces) frozen orange juice concentrate, thawed
- 7 medium firm bananas, sliced
- 1 can (20 ounces) crushed pineapple, undrained
- 1 bottle (20 ounces) lemon-lime soda, chilled

Direction

- In boiling water, dissolve the sugar. Put in pineapple, bananas and orange juice concentrate; whisk until blended. Whisk in soda then transfer into some small containers or a big container, then put in the freezer. Before serving, take out of the freezer for about 1 hour.

Nutrition Information

- Calories: 253 calories
- Sodium: 7mg sodium
- Fiber: 2g fiber)
- Total Carbohydrate: 64g carbohydrate (60g sugars
- Cholesterol: 0 cholesterol
- Protein: 1g protein.
- Total Fat: 0 fat (0 saturated fat)

345. Three Fruit Smoothies

Serving: 3 servings. | Prep: 10mins | Cook: 0mins | Ready in:

Ingredients

- 2 cartons (6 ounces each) fat-free reduced-sugar cherry-vanilla yogurt
- 1 small banana, halved
- 3/4 cup fresh or frozen blueberries
- 1 tablespoon honey
- 15 ice cubes

Direction

- Combine honey, blueberries, banana and yogurt in a blender; cover and blend till smooth. While blending, place in some ice cubes at a time till the mixture has the thickness you desire. Transfer into chilled glasses and serve at once.

Nutrition Information

- Calories: 130 calories
- Protein: 6g protein. Diabetic Exchanges: 2 fruit.
- Total Fat: 0 fat (0 saturated fat)
- Sodium: 69mg sodium
- Fiber: 2g fiber)
- Total Carbohydrate: 28g carbohydrate (24g sugars
- Cholesterol: 2mg cholesterol

346. Tipsy Iced Coffee

Serving: 8 servings. | Prep: 10mins | Cook: 0mins | Ready in:

Ingredients

- 4 cups strong brewed coffee
- 1/2 cup amaretto
- 1/4 cup plus 3 tablespoons sugar, divided
- 2/3 cup heavy whipping cream

Direction

- Whisk 1/4 cup of sugar, amaretto and coffee together in a big bowl. Let cool to room temperature.

- Pour into an 8-in. square dish and freeze for 1 hour. Use a fork to stir. Freeze for 2-3 more hours till frozen completely; after every 30 minutes, stir.
- In a meantime, beat cream in a small bowl till it begins to thicken. Add the leftover sugar then beat till it forms stiff peaks. Cover and place in the fridge till serving.
- Use a fork to stir the mixture then scoop into glasses to serve. Add whipped cream on top and immediately serve.

Nutrition Information

- Calories:
- Protein:
- Total Fat:
- Sodium:
- Fiber:
- Total Carbohydrate:
- Cholesterol:

347. Triple Berry Smoothies

Serving: 4 servings. | Prep: 15mins | Cook: 0mins | Ready in:

Ingredients

- 2 cups vanilla soy milk
- 1 teaspoon vanilla extract
- 6 ounces silken firm tofu
- 1 small banana, sliced and frozen
- 1/2 cup each frozen unsweetened raspberries, blackberries and strawberries
- 1 tablespoon sugar
- 4 tablespoons reduced-fat whipped topping

Direction

- Mix together sugar, berries, banana, tofu, vanilla and soy milk in a blender. Cover and blend until smooth, then transfer to cold glasses. Use whipped topping to decorate and serve promptly.

Nutrition Information

- Calories: 146 calories
- Cholesterol: 0 cholesterol
- Protein: 7g protein. Diabetic Exchanges: 1 fruit
- Total Fat: 3g fat (1g saturated fat)
- Sodium: 75mg sodium
- Fiber: 2g fiber)
- Total Carbohydrate: 22g carbohydrate (16g sugars

348. Tropical Fruit Punch

Serving: Makes 5 (1-1/2 cup) servings. | Prep: 5mins | Cook: | Ready in:

Ingredients

- 1 pkt. (makes 2 qt. drink) or 2 pkt. (makes 1 qt. drink each) CRYSTAL LIGHT Strawberry Orange Banana Flavor Drink Mix*
- 1 qt. (4 cups) cold pineapple-orange-banana juice blend
- 1 bottle (1 liter) club soda, chilled

Direction

- In a large glass or plastic pitcher, place drink mix then add juice blend. Stir to dissolve the drink mix. Store in the fridge till ready to serve.
- Transfer into a punch bowl right before serving. Add in club soda and stir. Pour over ice cubes to serve.

Nutrition Information

- Calories: 390
- Protein: 3 g
- Saturated Fat: 0 g
- Sodium: 85 mg

- Fiber: 0 g
- Total Carbohydrate: 97 g
- Total Fat: 0 g
- Sugar: 80 g
- Cholesterol: 0 mg

349. Tropical Fruit Slush

Serving: 12-14 servings. | Prep: 10mins | Cook: 5mins | Ready in:

Ingredients

- 3 cups water
- 1-1/2 cups sugar
- 6 medium ripe bananas, diced
- 2 cans (11 ounces each) mandarin oranges
- 1 can (20 ounces) crushed pineapple, undrained
- 1 can (12 ounces) frozen orange juice concentrate, thawed
- 1 jar (10 ounces) maraschino cherries, drained and halved
- 1/3 cup lemon juice

Direction

- Bring water and sugar in a saucepan to a boil, then cook and stir about 5 minutes. Take away from heat and allow to cool totally. Mix the leftover ingredients in a 4-quarter freezer container. Pour over the fruit with sugar water. Cover and freezer, while stirring one or two times, for minimum of 8 hours.
- Before serving, take out of the freezer about 20 minutes.

Nutrition Information

- Calories: 233 calories
- Fiber: 2g fiber)
- Total Carbohydrate: 61g carbohydrate (55g sugars
- Cholesterol: 0 cholesterol

- Protein: 1g protein.
- Total Fat: 0 fat (0 saturated fat)
- Sodium: 3mg sodium

350. Tropical Fruit Smoothies

Serving: 4 | Prep: 10mins | Cook: | Ready in:

Ingredients

- 1 (6 ounce) container apricot-mango, orange-mango, pina colada, or pineapple fat-free yogurt with artificial sweetener
- 1 cup fat-free milk
- 1 cup sliced fresh banana
- 1 cup sliced fresh mango or refrigerated mango slices
- 1 cup small ice cubes or crushed ice
- Sliced mango, lime wedges, or pineapple wedges (optional)

Direction

- Mix together 1 cup of mango, yogurt, banana and milk in a blender. Blend while covering till smooth. Put ice; cover then blend till smooth. Jazz it up with extra slices of mango or lime or pineapple wedges if you want.

Nutrition Information

- Calories: 98 calories;
- Total Fat: 0
- Fiber: 2
- Total Carbohydrate: 21
- Sugar: 16
- Protein: 4
- Saturated Fat: 0
- Sodium: 49
- Cholesterol: 2

351. Tropical Lime Punch

Serving: 20 servings (3/4 cup each). | Prep: 10mins | Cook: 0mins | Ready in:

Ingredients

- 4 cups unsweetened pineapple juice
- 1 can (12 ounces) frozen limeade concentrate, thawed
- 1/4 cup honey
- 1 vanilla bean
- 1 bottle (2 liters) lemon-flavored carbonated water
- 1 pint lemon sorbet
- 1 medium lemon, sliced
- 1 medium lime, sliced

Direction

- Combine honey, limeade concentrate and pineapple juice in a large pitcher. Split vanilla bean then scrape seeds into the pitcher; stir till combined. Cover and store in the fridge overnight.
- Place juice mixture into a punch bowl just before serving. Mix carbonated water in and scoop sorbet on top. Place in lime and lemon slices for garnish.

Nutrition Information

- Calories: 107 calories
- Protein: 0 protein.
- Total Fat: 0 fat (0 saturated fat)
- Sodium: 2mg sodium
- Fiber: 0 fiber)
- Total Carbohydrate: 27g carbohydrate (24g sugars
- Cholesterol: 0 cholesterol

352. Tropical Lime Smoothies

Serving: 3 servings. | Prep: 10mins | Cook: 0mins | Ready in:

Ingredients

- 1-1/4 cups milk
- 1/4 cup lime juice
- 1 pint coconut sorbet

Direction

- Mix all ingredients in a blender, then cover and blend until smooth. Transfer into cold glasses and serve promptly.

Nutrition Information

- Calories: 280 calories
- Cholesterol: 10mg cholesterol
- Protein: 3g protein.
- Total Fat: 13g fat (10g saturated fat)
- Sodium: 81mg sodium
- Fiber: 0 fiber)
- Total Carbohydrate: 40g carbohydrate (39g sugars

353. Tropical Punch

Serving: 40 servings (1/2-cup). | Prep: 15mins | Cook: 0mins | Ready in:

Ingredients

- 3 cups water
- 3/4 cup sugar
- 3 ripe bananas
- 1 can (46 ounces) pineapple juice, chilled
- 1-1/2 cups orange juice
- 1/4 cup lemon juice
- 1 bottle (2 liters) ginger ale, chilled

Direction

- Blend bananas, sugar and water together in a blender until the sugar dissolved and the mixture is smooth. Add to a big bowl; mix in the rest of the ingredients. Enjoy immediately.

Nutrition Information

- Calories: 63 calories
- Cholesterol: 0 cholesterol
- Protein: 0 protein.
- Total Fat: 0 fat (0 saturated fat)
- Sodium: 4mg sodium
- Fiber: 0 fiber)
- Total Carbohydrate: 16g carbohydrate (15g sugars

354. Vampire Killer

Serving: 8 servings. | Prep: 5mins | Cook: 0mins | Ready in:

Ingredients

- 1 serrano pepper, seeded and quartered
- 2 garlic cloves, crushed
- 1 lemon peel strip (2 inches)
- 1-1/2 cups vodka
- Ice
- GARNISH:
- Pickled baby beets

Direction

- In a plastic container or a large glass, place vodka, lemon peel, garlic and pepper. Cover and allow to stand for 1 week at room temperature.
- To prepare each serving: Add ice to fill 3/4 of a shaker. Place in 1-1/2 ounces of infused vodka then cover and shake till it forms condensation on the outside of the shaker, for 10-15 seconds. In a chilled martini glass, strain the drink and add a beet for garnish.

Nutrition Information

- Calories:
- Sodium:
- Fiber:
- Total Carbohydrate:
- Cholesterol:
- Protein:
- Total Fat:

355. Watermelon Cooler

Serving: 8 | Prep: 15mins | Cook: | Ready in:

Ingredients

- 1 small watermelon, seeded and cubed

Direction

- In a blender, blend watermelon cubes until smooth, then refrigerate before serving.

Nutrition Information

- Calories: 51 calories;
- Total Carbohydrate: 12.9
- Cholesterol: 0
- Total Fat: 0.3
- Protein: 1
- Sodium: 2

356. Watermelon Slush

Serving: 4 | Prep: | Cook: 10mins | Ready in:

Ingredients

- 3 cups diced watermelon
- 2 tablespoons lime juice
- 1 tablespoon sugar
- 1 cup crushed ice

- ½ cup water

Direction

- In a blender, process water, ice, sugar, lime juice and watermelon until smooth.

Nutrition Information

- Calories: 48 calories;
- Total Fat: 0
- Saturated Fat: 0
- Fiber: 0
- Cholesterol: 0
- Protein: 1
- Sodium: 2
- Total Carbohydrate: 12
- Sugar: 10

357. Watermelon Spritzer

Serving: 5 servings. | Prep: 5mins | Cook: 0mins | Ready in:

Ingredients

- 4 cups cubed seedless watermelon
- 3/4 cup frozen limeade concentrate, thawed
- 2-1/2 cups carbonated water
- Lime slices

Direction

- In a blender, add watermelon, then process, covered, until combined. Strain and throw away pulp, then remove juice to a pitcher. Stir in limeade concentrate and chill about 6 hours to overnight.
- Stir in carbonated water right before serving and use lime slices to decorate servings.

Nutrition Information

- Calories: 140 calories

- Total Fat: 0 fat (0 saturated fat)
- Sodium: 4mg sodium
- Fiber: 1g fiber)
- Total Carbohydrate: 38g carbohydrate (36g sugars
- Cholesterol: 0 cholesterol
- Protein: 0 protein.

358. Whipped Banana Latte

Serving: 5 servings. | Prep: 10mins | Cook: 0mins | Ready in:

Ingredients

- 1-1/2 cups cold strong brewed coffee
- 3/4 cup half-and-half cream
- 2 medium ripe bananas, frozen
- 1/2 cup ice cubes
- 1/4 cup sugar
- 2 tablespoons chocolate syrup

Direction

- In a blender, add all ingredients; cover and process till smooth for 15 seconds. Add into chilled glasses and immediately serve.

Nutrition Information

- Calories: 149 calories
- Cholesterol: 18mg cholesterol
- Protein: 2g protein.
- Total Fat: 4g fat (2g saturated fat)
- Sodium: 24mg sodium
- Fiber: 1g fiber)
- Total Carbohydrate: 27g carbohydrate (21g sugars

359. Whiskey Sour

Serving: 1 | Prep: 2mins | Cook: | Ready in:

Ingredients

- 2 fluid ounces whiskey
- 1 fluid ounce sweet and sour mix

Direction

- In a squat, old-fashioned glass, pour over ice cubes with sweet and sour and whiskey.

360. White Christmas Sangria

Serving: 21 servings (3-3/4 quarts). | Prep: 10mins | Cook: 0mins | Ready in:

Ingredients

- 6 cups white cranberry juice, chilled
- 3/4 cup thawed lemonade concentrate
- 3 bottles (25.4 ounces each) sparkling grape juice
- Pomegranate seeds and sliced grapefruit, oranges and kiwi, optional

Direction

- In a punch bowl, mix together lemonade concentrate and cranberry juice, then add in sparkling grape juice. Put in sliced fruit and pomegranate seeds, if wanted. Serve promptly.

Nutrition Information

- Calories: 110 calories
- Total Carbohydrate: 28g carbohydrate (28g sugars
- Cholesterol: 0 cholesterol
- Protein: 1g protein.
- Total Fat: 0 fat (0 saturated fat)
- Sodium: 5mg sodium
- Fiber: 0 fiber)

361. White Grape Punch

Serving: 6 quarts. | Prep: 15mins | Cook: 0mins | Ready in:

Ingredients

- 2 cans (12 ounces each) frozen apple juice concentrate, thawed
- 2 cans (11-1/2 ounces each) frozen white grape juice concentrate
- 6 cups cold water
- 12 cups lemon-lime soda (about 3 liters), chilled
- Lemon and lime slices

Direction

- Combine water, concentrate, white grape and apple juice concentrate in a large picher. Store in the fridge till serving.
- Transfer into a punch bowl or 2 pitchers right before serving. Add in soda and stir. Place lime and lemon slices on top.

Nutrition Information

- Calories: 109 calories
- Sodium: 17mg sodium
- Fiber: 0 fiber)
- Total Carbohydrate: 27g carbohydrate (27g sugars
- Cholesterol: 0 cholesterol
- Protein: 0 protein.
- Total Fat: 0 fat (0 saturated fat)

362. Wisconsin Whammer

Serving: 1 serving. | Prep: 5mins | Cook: 0mins | Ready in:

Ingredients

- 2 to 3 ice cubes
- 1/2 ounce orange juice

- 1/2 ounce brandy
- 2 teaspoons vodka
- 1 teaspoon amaretto

Direction

- In a tumbler or a mixing glass, add in ice then pour in amaretto, vodka, brandy and juice. Stir to combine. In a shot glass, strain the drink.

Nutrition Information

- Calories: 78 calories
- Total Fat: 0 fat (0 saturated fat)
- Sodium: 1mg sodium
- Fiber: 0 fiber)
- Total Carbohydrate: 3g carbohydrate (3g sugars
- Cholesterol: 0 cholesterol
- Protein: 0 protein.

363. Witches' Brew

Serving: 16 | Prep: 30mins | Cook: 10mins | Ready in:

Ingredients

- 1 (10 ounce) package frozen raspberries, thawed
- 2 1/2 cups cranberry juice
- 2 envelopes unflavored gelatin
- 2 liters ginger ale
- 2 liters sparkling apple cider (non-alcoholic)
- 6 gummi snakes candy

Direction

- For the frozen hand: Wash the outside of a rubber glove and rinse. Turn inside out and put aside. Combine cranberry juice and thawed raspberries in a 4-cup measuring cup.
- In a small saucepan, place 2 cups of raspberry mixture. Sprinkle over with gelatin and allow to stand for 2 minutes. Over low heat, warm and stir constantly to dissolve the gelatin. Return to the measuring cup of reserved raspberry mixture and mix.
- Add raspberry mixture to the inverted glove. Gather the glove top and use kitchen twine to securely tie. Let freeze for several days (if possible) or till solid.
- For serving: Discard the glove from the frozen hand carefully. Place it in a large punch bowl, leaning against the side, palm side facing up. Pour in sparkling cider and ginger ale. Place in gummy snakes for garnish.

Nutrition Information

- Calories: 156 calories;
- Total Fat: 0.1
- Sodium: 31
- Total Carbohydrate: 37.7
- Cholesterol: 0
- Protein: 0.9

364. Yogurt Breakfast Drink

Serving: 6 servings. | Prep: 5mins | Cook: 0mins | Ready in:

Ingredients

- 2 cups (16 ounces) vanilla yogurt
- 2 cups (16 ounces) peach yogurt
- 1/2 cup thawed orange juice concentrate
- 1/2 cup fat-free milk
- 2 cups ice cubes

Direction

- Mix the first four ingredients in a blender, then cover and blend until smooth. Put in ice cubes then cover and blend until smooth. Transfer into glasses and serve promptly.

Nutrition Information

- Calories: 166 calories

- Fiber: 0 fiber)
- Total Carbohydrate: 30g carbohydrate (0 sugars
- Cholesterol: 10mg cholesterol
- Protein: 8g protein. Diabetic Exchanges: 1 fruit
- Total Fat: 2g fat (1g saturated fat)
- Sodium: 100mg sodium

365. Yogurt Fruit Smoothies

Serving: 6 servings. | Prep: 10mins | Cook: 0mins | Ready in:

Ingredients

- 1 can (11-1/2 ounces) frozen strawberry breeze juice concentrate, thawed
- 1 cup (8 ounces) vanilla yogurt
- 1/2 cup milk
- 1 tablespoon honey
- 1 teaspoon vanilla extract
- 1 pint fresh strawberries, hulled
- 1 large banana, cut into chunks
- 1 cup chopped peeled fresh or frozen peaches
- 1 cup crushed ice

Direction

- In a blender, add 1/2 of all the ingredients; cover and blend till smooth, for 15 seconds. Transfer into chilled glasses. Do the process again. Serve at once.

Nutrition Information

- Calories: 225 calories
- Cholesterol: 4mg cholesterol
- Protein: 4g protein.
- Total Fat: 1g fat (1g saturated fat)
- Sodium: 38mg sodium
- Fiber: 2g fiber)
- Total Carbohydrate: 51g carbohydrate (42g sugars

Index

A
Ale 4,64
Almond 3,7,14
Angostura bitters 117
Apple 3,4,6,7,8,9,27,35,65,118
Apricot 3,9,10

B
Baking 89
Banana 3,4,5,6,10,11,12,13,14,16,19,21,22,27,33,34,44,91,100,125,126,130,142,146
Basil 3,15,16
Beer 3,16
Berry 3,4,5,6,12,16,17,18,19,20,31,46,50,72,79,88,99,119,122,142
Blackberry 3,21
Blueberry 3,5,22,23,24,40,93
Bran 3,7,9,21,25
Butter 3,5,26,27,91,99,100,101

C
Carrot 6,132
Champ 3,4,5,28,29,64,89,104,106,110,113,122
Cheese 6,114
Cherry 3,30,31
Chocolate 3,4,5,14,30,33,55,58,92
Cider 3,6,8,118,122
Cinnamon 3,35,53
Cocktail 3,5,6,15,106,110,116

Coffee 3,4,5,6,11,32,33,38,39,54,75,93,141
Cola 3,5,39,94
Cranberry 3,4,5,29,41,42,43,44,45,52,70,108
Cream 3,4,5,26,46,47,48,49,93,110
Cucumber 4,50

E
Egg 3,4,5,32,46,51,52,71,92,102

F
Fat 7,8,9,10,11,12,13,14,15,16,17,18,19,20,21,22,23,24,25,26,27,28,29,30,31,32,33,34,35,36,37,38,39,40,41,42,43,44,45,46,47,48,49,50,51,52,53,54,55,56,57,58,59,60,61,62,63,64,65,66,67,68,69,70,71,72,73,74,75,76,77,78,79,80,81,82,83,84,85,86,87,88,89,90,91,92,93,94,95,96,97,98,99,100,101,102,103,104,105,106,107,108,109,110,111,112,113,114,115,116,117,118,119,120,121,122,123,124,125,126,127,128,129,130,131,132,133,134,135,136,137,138,139,140,141,142,143,144,145,146,147,148,149
Fruit 3,4,5,6,17,22,53,55,56,57,60,61,62,63,64,66,91,102,108,121,125,133,138,141,142,143,149

G
Gin 4,5,64,65,106,130
Grapefruit 5,104

H
Honey 4,72,73,75

J
Jelly 5,101
Jus 67,126

K
Kale 4,65

L
Lemon

3,4,5,6,7,21,32,37,41,44,51,54,55,56,62,68,71,76,77,79,80,85,87,88,90,99,110,114,119,127,128,135,147

Lime 4,5,6,20,25,37,47,51,73,81,82,83,84,129,140,144,146

M

Mandarin 4,47

Mango 3,5,6,23,86,129,136

Melon 4,6,50,76,130

Milk 3,4,5,6,11,14,23,28,38,50,62,72,82,92,95,102,133,140

Mint 3,4,5,36,62,75,76,87,88,90,91,111

N

Nut 3,5,7,8,9,10,11,12,13,14,15,16,17,18,19,20,21,22,23,24,25,26,27,28,29,30,31,32,33,34,35,36,37,38,39,40,41,42,43,44,45,46,47,48,49,50,51,52,53,54,55,56,57,58,59,60,61,62,63,64,65,66,67,68,69,70,71,72,73,74,75,76,77,78,79,80,81,82,83,84,85,86,87,88,89,90,91,92,93,94,95,96,97,98,99,100,101,102,103,104,105,106,107,108,109,110,111,112,113,114,115,116,117,118,119,120,121,122,123,124,125,126,127,128,129,130,131,132,133,134,135,136,137,138,139,140,141,142,143,144,145,146,147,148,149

O

Orange 3,4,5,6,19,24,28,38,42,48,49,57,58,66,80,88,93,94,95,96,97,103,105,116,122,135,138,142

P

Peach 3,4,5,6,10,65,96,97,98,99,100,121,130,133,140

Pear 5,101

Peel 24,72,118

Pepper 5,102

Pickle 145

Pie 3,9

Pineapple 3,4,5,6,13,58,80,94,95,103,104,123,131

Pomegranate 4,5,42,106,111,147

Pumpkin 5,107

R

Raspberry 3,4,5,6,16,41,43,55,87,109,110,111,112,137

Rhubarb 4,5,6,59,85,114,115

S

Seeds 19

Soda 5,93

Spinach 19

Strawberry 3,4,5,6,14,49,59,77,90,96,100,125,126,127,128,129,130,131,132,133,139,142

Sugar 6,19,20,28,36,37,38,48,50,52,62,72,75,81,112,123,129,132,133,138,143,146

Syrup 4,41,54

T

Tea 3,4,5,6,7,16,36,38,41,70,74,75,76,77,80,83,86,87,109,112,113,123,133,134,136,137,138

Tequila 6,139

Thyme 4,68

Tomato 3,6,15,124

W

Watermelon 5,6,109,145,146

Wine 5,6,98,105,116

Worcestershire sauce 15,53,124

Conclusion

Thank you again for downloading this book!

I hope you enjoyed reading about my book!

If you enjoyed this book, please take the time to share your thoughts and post a review on Amazon. It'd be greatly appreciated!

Write me an honest review about the book – I truly value your opinion and thoughts and I will incorporate them into my next book, which is already underway.

Thank you!

If you have any questions, **feel free to contact at:** *publishing@crumblerecipes.com*

Tracy Yost

crumblerecipes.com

www.ingramcontent.com/pod-product-compliance
Lightning Source LLC
LaVergne TN
LVHW081554230125
801996LV00016B/683